من دے شکر گذار ہوں ست گورد حضور

بابا ساون سنگهہ جی سانگھ جی دے لیکھا

"In the service of my Guru, the perfect Master, Hazur Baba Sawan Singh Ji...."

The Urdu words reproduced above were noted by Maharaj Ji across his desk diary
during the last day he worked in his office.

Published by:

Sewa Singh, Secretary
Radha Soami Satsang Beas
Dera Baba Jaimal Singh
Dist. Amritsar 143204
Punjab, India

Colour separations by Evergreen Colour Separation (Scanning) Co. Ltd., Hong Kong.
Printed and bound by South Sea International Press Ltd., Hong Kong

CONTENTS

PREFACE

MAN'S DESIRE TO KNOW THE DIVINE has taken him to the extremes of knowledge and sensory experience. Yet whilst the creation may have matured in scientific and material means, most people would agree that we are as far from understanding the divine as we ever were. The fault lies as much in our lack of objectivity as in the means we adopt. Ironically, although it is in our nature to learn from other human beings in every other sphere, in spiritual matters we think we are self-sufficient. When trying to understand what lies beyond the physical, our ego—that particularly human combination of mental arrogance and spiritual immaturity—prevents us from seeing our limitations, even though it would be more natural to learn from a peer.

As in every sphere, divine knowledge can best be acquired by observing practical examples. Without a living example in front of us, we can get lost in the complexities of concepts and theories, whereas a practical example of what we seek can point us straight to our goal. Such was Hazur Maharaj Charan Singh—our friend, our teacher, divine guide and incomparable example. The influence of an enlightened human being such as he clearly extended beyond the normal boundaries of human experience. The spiritual energy surrounding him touched the highest recesses of the hearts of all who came in contact with him. As he uplifted our consciousness, Maharaj Ji awakened us to the possibility of genuine knowledge of God. Seeing the harmony and perfect balance of his person, we had a burning desire to become like him.

Our hunger to know all about Maharaj Ji, therefore, was insatiable. To be with him was to be with one's best friend in a garden of tranquillity and understanding. Nothing we knew in life was sweeter—so, with our immature understanding, we tried to learn his truth. We attempted to listen carefully to every word he spoke and digest its meaning. We watched every movement, gesture and expression, trying to carry with us the memory of his face and his presence. There was nothing about our beloved teacher that was not important to us.

Who ever thought about the day when it would no longer be possible to be in the presence of this beautiful human being? Who could imagine the import of that first day of June in 1990 when, with an unequivocal instruction to his youthful successor to take from his hands both his spiritual and temporal work, he simply shrugged off the limitations of his body and merged back into that limitless ocean of love from which he had come?

Learning of his passing, his followers reacted at first with disbelief and dismay, then with anguish and grief. Yet without us realizing it, he had prepared us for this inconceivable change. He had prepared his sangat so thoroughly that it is now possible to look back on the decade since that day and marvel, filled with gratitude at the way he softened our loss.

Throughout the years he had taught that the real guide or Master is the spiritual form, the Shabd form. In the Shabd form, our Master never leaves us. Maharaj Ji used to tell us: *"In each one of you a light is shining, and from within it the most melodious music is pouring forth. If you experience this inner light, or darshan, and are able to catch hold of the sound of the music, your worldly attachments and love will leave you, and instead you will become attached to the Lord."* Though it is nature's plan that the mystic saints, like the rest of us, must eventually leave the body, as the Comforter—that radiant and melodious power of Shabd that Maharaj Ji put us in touch with—they remain forever within us, showing us the way back to our true home.

Perhaps it was only by Maharaj Ji's passing from the physical plane that we could realize the depths of his message. Only by his leaving us could we experience the bittersweet nature of this affair of the heart with the living Master! All those years, the arrows of his love had been piercing us. But it was only when he was physically gone that we felt the pain and realized how deep those wounds of love had become. Such is the power of the Master's attraction: the need to consummate that love, to lose our insipid personalities and become one with him again becomes an overwhelming force. It can only end in one way. That love must make us turn towards him inwardly. Great Master put it very beautifully: *"The Masters become a bridge for us to cross. By loving a perfect Master, our soul eventually comes to love the formless and indescribable one and only God. Although the Lord, like electricity, pervades everywhere, the Master is the point where he shines out as light."*

Maharaj Ji once wrote to a dear friend the following words describing the indissoluble bond between Master and disciple: *"I know what it means to you to be out of Dera, but one has to attend to one's duties. You yourself have written in the Urdu couplet: 'I am going out of your world. Please arise and accept my goodbye.' It is very difficult, rather it is impossible, to get out of Maharaj Ji's world* [he is here speaking of his own Master] *because he is omnipotent and omnipresent—everywhere—wherever we may be. Once we are accepted, He is with us always. His jurisdiction is not confined to India alone but rather extends to the next world and beyond. So in spite of your best efforts, you will not be able to get out of his world, and the question of accepting 'goodbye' does not arise. As we are so roped together, ultimately there is one shepherd and one fold. This has to be so, whether you like it or not."*

No book can provide more than a sketch of who and what Maharaj Ji was. No photograph can show the nature of a glance from his eyes, the sweet sound of his voice, the power of his presence, the infectious quality of his laugh and smile. Yet as fragrance evokes a flower, so do images quicken the heart's memory. It is our earnest hope that the wide range of photographs included in this book will serve to recall the unique relationship that each one of us experienced with this extraordinary being.

The book is organized in six chapters. The first covers Maharaj Ji's early years—his youth, education, profession, and early married life. These were the years when he established friendships and relationships that would remain with him throughout his life, and when he began his journey as a young disciple on the inner path. Most crucially, it was the period of his formative relationship with the Great Master, his paternal grandfather, who in all matters, both practical and spiritual, was the keystone of his life.

In the second chapter comes the great watershed of successorship, of his taking over the reins from Sardar Bahadur Ji Maharaj of that awesome seva which, only three years previously, had been in the sacred hands of his own Master. We see the obedient disciple almost crushed under his sense of unworthiness, and we see the emergent Master making radical and dynamic changes to safeguard the integrity of his predecessors' work.

The third chapter gives some sense of Maharaj Ji's countless and extensive travels in India and abroad as he carried the message of the Shabd to his marked souls, far and wide. And in the fourth chapter, we see the visionary and untiring sevadar living and working at the Dera. From a small community of a few hundred permanent residents, he expanded the colony to a humming township with adequate amenities to shelter and feed the vast numbers that came there regularly by the time he left this earth. Both chapters give a glimpse of the extent and diversity of his regular duties wherever he was. Functioning as spiritual Master to an ever-growing sangat, and as patron of the society he had created for administrative purposes, he kept a back-breaking daily schedule that staggers the imagination.

In Chapter Five we focus on the man. Over some forty years we see him as a photographer, traveller, enthusiast; as a family man, son, husband, father, uncle and grandfather; and we see him as a loyal and much-loved friend. Here we note his boundless zest for life, his exuberance and his wide-ranging interests. Notwithstanding his great responsibilities, we find him playful, full of good humour, laughter and fun.

The album finally ends with images that point to his timeless legacy: the gift of love that is inseparable and indistinguishable from his gift of the Shabd. Through his satsangs he revealed its value to us. Through his selfless service he demonstrated its power and put us in touch with it. Through his very nature—his overflowing grace and compassion—he showered us with that love so we too could make it ours.

As he lives on—a bright and shining light within all who loved him—this book is placed before him. It is a tribute to him: saint among saints, man of God, friend, beloved, most precious human being. There are no words to thank our beloved Hazur Maharaj Ji. But we can recall his response when asked if there was any gift we could give to him. He said: *"The best gift you can give your Master is the gift of meditation. Nothing else matters."*

RADHA SOAMI SATSANG BEAS
JANUARY 2000

A NOTE TO THE READER

All direct quotations from Maharaj Ji are rendered in a brown colour, and those in green are his own handwriting. All other quotations and narrative text are in black.

Legacy of Love

Charan Sĭ́
Sea-Ben

CHAPTER ONE

The Early Years

Maharaj Charan Singh was born on December 12, 1916, in his maternal home at Moga in the erstwhile Ferozepur district of Punjab. His father, Sardar Harbans Singh Grewal, was the youngest son of Maharaj Sawan Singh Ji, who was affectionately known as Great Master, *Badé Maharaj Ji*. Maharaj Sawan Singh was thus both the head of their family and their spiritual Master. When his grandson Charan was first presented to him, he commented to those present that the child was greatly blessed—he would have spiritual wealth in abundance, and he would also enrich others from that wealth.

Maharaj Ji was the eldest of seven children—three boys and four girls. His brother, Purshotam (or Shoti as he was better known), later served in the Indian army and sought early release at the rank of captain to help Maharaj Ji with family matters after his appointment as Master. His youngest brother, Jagjit, died of an illness in 1948 while still in his teens. His four sisters, Satnam Kaur, Gurnam Kaur, Mohinder Kaur and Baljinder Kaur, had great respect for the two elder brothers and throughout their lives were always very protective of them.

The children spent their earliest years at the family farm in Sikanderpur, near Sirsa in Haryana, which Great Master had established through years of hard work. Since there were no educational facilities near the farm, Great Master asked that the children be sent to live with him at the Dera from where they would be able to attend school. Dera thus became Maharaj Ji's home from a very early age—so much so that Bibi Ralli, a devoted sevadar assigned to look after the two boys, once commented that for many years Maharaj Ji even thought Great Master was his father.

During these formative years, a strong bond developed between the young Charan and his grandfather. The two brothers attended primary school in Balsarai, a village hardly two kilometres from the Dera, and secondary school in Baba Bakala, some six kilometres away. Great Master gave them their first lessons in spirituality, teaching them at a tender age to sit quietly alone in a closed room for fifteen minutes daily. Bibi Ralli was charged to ensure that this was done every day and that they also attended satsang. Known for her strictness, she no doubt saw that Great Master's orders were complied with to the letter.

The young Charan's love and respect for his grandfather is evident from the many stories he would later recount. On one occasion the Great Master asked him what he would like to be when he grew up: would he want to be an ordinary son, a bad son or a good son. When Maharaj Ji asked what the difference was between the three, Great Master explained that an ordinary son neither increases nor decreases his inheritance, a bad son squanders his inheritance, whereas a good son puts his inheritance to proper use, increases it and uses it to help others. The young teenager replied that whilst everyone wants to be a good son, since everything was in Great Master's hands, it was entirely up to him to mold him in whichever way he pleased. This absolute trust and faith in his Master—the way in which he let Great Master shape him in every respect—was characteristic of him throughout his life.

After completing secondary school in 1933, he studied for what was then known as the Intermediate exams in D.A.V. College, Jalandhar, and Randhir College, Kapurthala. At that time he stayed with his tutor, Professor Jagmohan Lal, (the same professor who later served him as a sevadar, helping him with overseas correspondence). Throughout his college years, he pursued several hobbies: he enjoyed photography, an interest that would develop into a lifelong hobby, and sports—becoming an accomplished tennis player by the time he studied law. Loyal and steady by nature, the friendships he formed during his student years would last him throughout his life.

While living in the college hostel, he would visit the Dera for weekends and holidays. Along with several friends, he helped form the Sawan Service League, a group of young men keen to be of service to the Great Master. They chose office bearers from among themselves, and Maharaj Ji was selected to be the president and take charge of the administrative duties. Since there was no electricity in those days at the Dera, he was also regularly given the seva of fanning Great Master during satsang in the intense heat of the summer months.

At the age of 22 he completed his B.A. degree at Gordon College, Rawalpindi, and went on to study law at Punjab University, Lahore. After receiving his LL.B. degree in 1942, he started to build his own practice as a lawyer in the town of Sirsa, near the family farm. As was customary in those days, he handed over whatever he earned to his grandfather as the head of the family. Great Master would then return to him what he decided appropriate to meet his daily expenses, give some money to the Dera in seva, and keep the rest for him as savings.

In 1943 Great Master arranged his marriage to Harjeet Kaur, the daughter of Rao Bahadur Shiv Dhyan Singh, a devoted satsangi from the state of Pisawa, in Uttar Pradesh. Great Master himself led the marriage party to Pisawa when the wedding took place in November of the following year.

By the end of September 1947, Great Master had become very sick and had to be taken to Amritsar for treatment. From October 1947, Maharaj Ji remained with him, serving him constantly until he passed away on April 2, 1948. Throughout these six months he left his grandfather for only two or three days, when he was asked by him to receive Dr Pierre Schmidt on his arrival from Switzerland and bring him to the Dera.

It was during this period that news came that he had been officially selected for a post in the judiciary. Great Master responded by asking him what purpose it would serve for him to become a judge. Rather, he said, he should wait and see what Baba Ji's order for him was. He then told him that since his father's health was failing and Shoti was away in the army, he should give up practising law and help his father with the family farm.

He accepted the Great Master's guidance without question and gave up his practice and independent life in Sirsa. With no idea of what lay in store for him only a few years ahead, he left his active life as a young and successful lawyer, moved back to Sikanderpur, and applied himself to running the family farm.

Three years later, at the age of thirty-five, Maharaj Ji was appointed Master by Sardar Bahadur Ji. By then, Maharaj Ji had three small children to care for—Nirmaljit Kaur (Nimmi), Jasbir (Cuckoo), and Ranbir (Rana). His brother Shoti took over the practical work of providing for the joint family, leaving Maharaj Ji free to give his full attention to the great responsibility that mastership had now placed on his shoulders.

1922–23. Taken in Beas when Maharaj Ji was six years old.
Front, L-R: The young Harcharan (Charan) and his brother Purshotam (Shoti).
Rear, L-R: Satnam Singh, Gurdial Singh Claire and Jaswant Singh Claire (nephew and son of Sardar Bahadur Ji).

G. T. B. KHALSA HIGH SCHOOL, BABA BAKALA
TENTH CLASS 1932–33

At sixteen years old.

Maharaj Ji, recalling his initiation —

I was initiated in 1933 [when I was seventeen years old]. There were three or four of us as students who were always asking my aunt, Bhua Ji, to request the Great Master to initiate us, but he said: "Unless you pass the matriculation examination, I will not initiate you."

So I worked very hard, but still I only got a second division. But the best division I got when he initiated me. The day our results came out—we had forgotten about initiation and were playing football outside somewhere—my aunt sent for me with the message: "Maharaj Ji is calling you for initiation." We came running and got initiated. We were initiated in the Nam Ghar—there were barely seventy or eighty people there, maybe even less. The man who was sitting by my side at the initiation was a tonga driver. His name is Hari Singh. His brother, Jagat Singh, was sitting on my other side. They are both still living, the oldest tonga drivers in the Dera. They live in a nearby village and are still plying their tongas here.

Continuing in a lighter vein —

*N*aturally when you are first initiated, you are anxious to sit in meditation. You think that you will go on sitting in meditation for the whole day, probably. After initiation another friend and I—you all know him, but I will not name him—went to the Guest House where we used to stay sometimes for studying, and we sat in meditation. The bell rang for satsang at four o'clock in the afternoon (there was no siren in those days) and it sounded just like a church bell. Sometimes it is still used here.

When he got up from meditation, he asked me: "Did you hear anything?"

I said: "No."

He said: "I heard the bell!"

I said: "When?"

He said: "Just now I heard the bell."

I said: "You are more fortunate than me. Let us go to satsang!"

D.A.V. College, Jalandhar. Intermediate Economics Group. 1934–35

One should never worry about one's karmas. A student should only worry about working hard, about doing his best, and then leave it to the Lord. We have to do our duty; we have to do our best. We must not deceive ourselves, we must be honest with ourselves and attend to our meditation. Then leave it to the Father to do whatever he feels like. How he arranges things—that is his job. We shouldn't try to regulate how he does things. We must regulate our own part, not his part.

TUTORIAL GROUP 'J'
Randhir College, Kapurthala
1936 – 37

Outgoing class of '37 on the occasion of a farewell gathering. *Front row, L-R:* Maharaj Ji, not known, Sardar Behl Singh (Principal), Prof. Jagmohan Lal (Vice Principal), Ravi Bhatnagar, others not known.

He used to describe himself often as an average student when it came to academic subjects. He had various hobbies, including photography and several sports, and he enjoyed going to the cinema. At the end of his intermediate year at D.A.V. College, Jalandhar, he failed in Persian and when asked by the Great Master what had happened, he pointed out that a particular film, a favourite of the time, had been showing during the two weeks of the exams and he had seen it every night! Professor Jagmohan Lal suggested it was simply a matter of some tutorial support, and that the boy should be sent to him in Kapurtala so he could provide that support. Persian was a compulsory subject and the system was such that if one didn't pass in all subjects, one would be failed overall. So Maharaj Ji went to Randhir College in Kapurtala and studied under the tutelage of Prof. Jagmohan Lal, before going on to do an Arts degree at Gordon College, Rawalpindi.

1936–37

To lead a good, pure, moral life in youth needs
the courage, bravery and resolve of a prophet.
Maharaj Jagat Singh

Maharaj Ji's photograph of the satsang ghar under construction in 1936, taken with his four-rupee box camera. The short tower on the left was a temporary water tower which was used during construction and then demolished when the building was completed.

"Communal Feast." Taken by Maharaj Ji in Rawalpindi in 1937, this photograph won a prize in a contest held by the Indian edition of *The Illustrated Weekly.*

𝒫hotography was just my hobby. I started when I was in Rawalpindi studying for my B.A. Another class fellow had a camera. Naturally I was also tempted to have one. In those days you could buy a box camera for four rupees; and you didn't have to know much except to press the shutter and nothing else; everything was within focus. So I started with that. Then this hobby developed due to association with others whose interest was photography—as we are always influenced by the company we keep. The Mahatta brothers were good friends of mine, so this association with them naturally developed a deep-rooted hobby.

THE DRAMATIC CLUB
GORDON COLLEGE, RAWALPINDI
1938–39

As a college student, Maharaj Ji enjoyed amateur dramatics. Once, in a college variety show, he played his friend's wife. Concealed from head to toe under a burqa, he created great merriment when, just as the play was about to finish, he lifted the veil of the all-enveloping gown to reveal his bearded face.

Gordon College, Rawalpindi. 1938

MR. F. H. SHAH'S TUTORIAL GROUP
Law College, Lahore 1940–41

If we live in His will and if we are grateful to Him for whatever He has given us, then we feel extremely happy and light.

With an overseas visitor and Harmohinder Ahuja on the upstairs terrace of the house that was later occupied by Dr Stone. The river Beas is in the background.

Maharaj Ji (fifth from left) with Harmohinder Ahuja (holding hat), Shoti and friends in Dalhousie. 1940

With Jeevan Batta. 1939

Ellesmere, Dalhousie. *L-R:* Harmohinder Ahuja, Maharaj Ji, Yograj Oberoi, Shoti, Amrit Anand. 1940

He was the most loyal of friends and his friends were friends for life. No matter what his responsibilities were, he always found time for them. As the years passed, many of them became devoted sevadars and in their later years, served with him at the Dera.

On the occasion of Iqbal Dharmani's marriage at his ancestral home in Anandpur Sahib. *L-R:* Bhagwan (Bibi Ralli's nephew), Shoti, Iqbal, Maharaj Ji, Janak Puri. 1941

Great Master leaving satsang. Rai Sahib (known by all as "Deputy") Harnarain is sitting to his left. Maharaj Ji is standing on the left dashboard, Shoti on the right dashboard, Sardar Bhagat Singh (Sardar Bahadur Ji's brother) is in the front passenger seat with Damodar, the driver.

With Great Master and Bibi Rakhi, Bibi Ralli and Bibi Lajjo.

Great Master was such a great personality. What we read is nothing, what we know is nothing. It was to be seen to experience what he was—I mean, words can't describe his love and affection and his way of dealing with people with so much patience and the way he served the sangat. He created from scrap the whole colony, the whole Dera, and he spread his teachings in all corners of the world. The less said the better! I have not been able to find any correct description by any author, who could really describe what he was, and neither do I think anybody can describe him.

Dalhousie. *Standing, L-R:* S. S. Bhandari, L. C. Dharmani, Rai Sahib Harnarain, Prof. Guranlal, Prof. Bhatnagar, Gurdayal Dharmani. *Seated, L-R:* R. C. Mehta, Shoti, Great Master, Maharaj Ji. 1942

The Sawan Service League was formed sometime during the early 1940s and given its name by Dr Johnson. A number of young men, including Maharaj Ji, Shoti, L. C. Dharmani and S. S. Bhandari, got together and organized themselves into a working group to be helpful to the Great Master in looking after the colony. Some helped with the arrangements for visitors, some with the langar—carrying dal, chapatis and utensils or tea to wherever they were needed, some helped with traffic control. They decided amongst themselves who would do what and appointed each other to different positions such as president and secretary. All took turns doing the different sevas, several of which were later reflected in their duties as permanent sevadars some thirty years later. Maharaj Ji was their President, responsible for the administration of the League. They had a small office, not far from today's library building, which Sardar Bahadur Ji, passing by and seeing this group of young, enthusiastic men enjoying themselves, would sometimes call the 'worthless' or 'work-less' office to tease them.

In Dalhousie, wearing a Sawan Service League medal given to him and some of his friends by Great Master on the occasion of Great Master's birthday. 1942

In Ellesmere, Dalhousie. 1941–42

In later years Maharaj Ji often recalled his early years with Great Master —

*H*e was the most relaxed man I have ever seen in my life. I've never seen anybody so relaxed in a gathering. The most difficult thing is to relax in a gathering of lakhs. And I have seen him cutting jokes in the satsang. And not only laughing, but making people laugh. He was the most relaxed person under every situation.

*W*orldly things—we always discussed everything with him. Actually, not discussed—we listened. We received orders and obeyed them; no questions had to be put. For everything else, we kept quiet.

On the roof terrace of Dr Johnson's house at the Dera with Mrs Colleen, a spirited, fun-loving Swiss lady satsangi who taught French and German in India. *Front, L-R:* Jaswant Singh Claire (Sardar Bahadur Ji's son), Ravi Bhatnagar (in black cap), Janak Puri (in overcoat), Harmohinder Ahuja, Mrs Colleen (kneeling with stick), Maharaj Ji (with scarf), not known, Darshan Singh, Bhagwan, Randhir (the poet and entertainer of the group), Sohan Singh Bhandari. *On the stairs, from top coming down:* Prof. Bhatnagar (on right), A. N. Mehta (on left), Shoti (with scarf), not known, Guranlal (on left), L. C. Dharmani (on right). Early '40s

Standing, L-R: L. C. Dharmani (at extreme left), next four not known, Maharaj Ji (centre, wearing coat), Gurbaksh Singh Randhir, Gopal Singh Lattha, Hardyal, S. S. Bhandari (in dark coat), next two not known, Diwan Ali.
Seated, L-R: Ravi Bhatnagar, Vishwanath, Gurdial, Great Master, Shoti, not known.

LAW COLLEGE LAHORE

MONTMORENCY HALL TENNIS TOURNMENT
1941–42

Tennis was his favourite sport and he was a good player. He did well in college and played fast and aggressive at net!

As a law student. 1942

I think Great Master told me to do law, to be very frank. I don't recollect I had any aptitude—even for study. I was very fond of sports. My school is very near, about three or four miles from here. Even my subjects were selected by the Great Master. We didn't know what were the subjects we should choose. He said: "You better select arts subjects." So I did arts. Then, for my B.A. I selected my own subjects. After that he told me, "You better join law college." So I joined law college. It was so simple.

In Kashmir with Harmohinder (centre) and another friend. 1944

All humans are the same, whether they are satsangis or non-satsangis. Some non-satsangis are excellent people, wonderful people to deal with, whilst some satsangis—you may shudder to talk to them even. We have to select our own atmosphere. We have to use our sense of discrimination about whom to mix with and whom not to mix with. It should make no difference whether they are satsangis or not satsangis.

Manasbal Lake, Kashmir. The child with Maharaj Ji is R.C. Mehta's son, Ishi; R.C. Mehta on right (with hat), Harmohinder Ahuja beside him.

*W*e are bound to each other by karmic strings—we come here to settle our karmic debits and credits. We come to this world as parents and children, as friends and relatives, but as soon as our karmic accounts for this life are settled we depart, each going his own way. This world is like an inn where we all gather together for the night, but at daybreak we all go our different ways. We are like birds that take shelter in a tree in the evening, but with the first light of dawn, each flies off on its own way.

Maharaj Ji (walking toward camera) on a trek to Konsarnag Lake at 12,000 ft. Kashmir. June 1944

*I*f it is your destiny—mountain climbing—how can you avoid it? You are happy in climbing mountains, you want to be adventurous and you like hiking, what is the harm? Some people like to swim in the sea: for a layman like me, it would be very dangerous—someone who doesn't know swimming! But, those who know swimming—they keep jumping like fish.

With R. N. Mehta.

The young lawyer. 1943–44

*W*ell, being a lawyer is a very difficult job I must say—having gone through it myself—being an attorney myself. I know it's a very painful thing—to know an innocent person is held guilty or someone rightly accused gets free. I tell you, when I just entered law, my client told me that he was absolutely innocent and I even went out of my way to get him acquitted. You have to use all your skills with the court and they sometimes favour you. But when he was acquitted, I came to know he was really guilty. Well I felt very, very bad. I told the Great Master this had happened and that it pained me very much that he had lied to me. My Master told me, "Remember one thing, never ask any client whether he is guilty or not guilty, just confine yourself to the file, to the evidence, and fight your case from the file, from the evidence. Your client is your file, the evidence before you. Don't worry about any personality." I can pass on the same advice to you.

Maharaj Ji, R. C. Mehta, Shoti and Harbans Singh of Hoshiarpur during Maharaj Ji's wedding festivities at Pisawa. November 1944

With Great Master and his father-in-law, Rao Sahib Shiv Dhyan Singh.

Maharaj Ji's bride was from the small state of Pisawa in Uttar Pradesh, situated some considerable distance from the Dera. Great Master himself led the *baraat*, a large party of the groom's family and friends, to Pisawa Fort where the formalities and celebrations took place over several days. The actual wedding ceremony took place in the ladies' quarters of the fort and was conducted by Great Master who started it by speaking on some verses from the Adi Granth. Sardar Bhagat Singh, cousin of Sardar Bahadur Ji, then explained the difference between the Hindu and Sikh forms of marriage since the bride was from a Hindu background and the groom's family were Sikh. The formal ceremony was concluded with the ladies from the bride's family garlanding the groom.

November 26, 1944

Speaking in later years about the institution of marriage —

*M*arriage is an obligation, a great responsibility to so many people. Love alone doesn't make a marriage a success unless understanding is there. Love must be based on understanding.

*I*f the understanding is on both sides, then there's no conflict. It's a give and take on both sides, it should be the general attitude of the couple to adjust. If the adjustment is there, then there is no problem. Otherwise, very small things become big issues. One has to handle situations very carefully, very lovingly.

Great Master conducting Maharaj Ji's wedding ceremony at Pisawa. Shoti at Maharaj Ji's left, Ram Kishan Singh (bride's brother) to his left, Sardar Bachint Singh (Great Master's elder son) behind them, Sardar Bhagat Singh (front row, facing camera), Harmohinder to his right (wearing hat), Prof. Jagmohan Lal to his right (behind the pole), Sardar Harbans Singh (Maharaj Ji's father) behind Sardar Bhagat Singh.

Once we have taken that alliance, once we have taken that obligation, we must discharge it no matter what comes. So many storms come in marriages, so many differences come, but if we have one aim—not to leave each other—they just go. We have to live together for the sake of those responsibilities and obligations we have taken on our shoulders. That should keep us tied down together—not the infatuation, which sooner or later will evaporate, will vanish.

Love means that which lasts forever. It doesn't diminish. It always grows and grows and grows and grows. That is not love that today we feel, and tomorrow we feel "I don't love them anymore." If love comes, it never goes. If it goes, it is not love.

Maharaj Ji on his wedding day at Pisawa Fort. *Standing, L-R:* Banke Rai (a lawyer colleague), Bhagwan, R.N. Mehta, R. C. Mehta, Harmohinder Ahuja, Captain Lal Singh (Maharaj Ji's uncle and ADC to the Viceroy of India), Gopa (with camera), Janak Puri (behind him), Maharaj Ji, Dev Prakash, Ajit, Shoti, not known, Mohinder, Kola, Gurbaksh Aggarwal (son of Gulwant Rai).
Seated, L-R: not known, Balwant, Hardyal, Darshan, Randhir, Hardeep (foreground), Harbans (in dark coat), Gurdial.

In Pisawa at the time of his marriage. *L-R:* R. C. Mehta, Shoti, Maharaj Ji, R. N. Mehta.

With Great Master (seated), his father Sardar Harbans Singh (to his right) and his father-in-law Rao Sahib Shiv Dhyan Singh (to his left).

*T*here can be no ego before a person who you love because love creates that humility in us. We try to become another being, we try to lose our own identity, our individuality, and we try to become another being. That is love. So, automatically we are filled with humility.

Visiting Satguru Partap Singh Ji at the Namdhari farm in Sirsa with Great Master. Sardar Bachint Singh at extreme left, Maharaj Ji's father sitting behind Maharaj Ji.

With Dr Pierre Schmidt who came to India to attend to Great Master in his last months in 1948.

I only started as a lawyer in '43 in right earnest because in 1942, I had just qualified, and for the first few months I was trying to prepare myself. From 1943 to '46, and half '47, I earnestly attended to it. Then Great Master was ill so I joined him, and I remained with him till his last days. Then for six, seven months I was not in a mood even to go to the courts, and by the time I started again, my father asked me to join him at the farm. Great Master told me while going: "Your father is failing in health every day. You better go to the farm now. You have had enough experience of law."

I joined him in the beginning of '49 and stayed with him till I was called here in 1951. The farm didn't interest me. Being a lawyer and being so much involved in the court work and all the judiciary, the local clubs and all that, and then to sit on the farm without any company or anything—it was a great trial. I knew nothing about the farm. But, I was there all through. My father said your presence is required more than your knowledge about farming. My presence was there all through.

With his wife, Harjeet, in Sirsa. 1945

Harmohinder's wedding. Maharaj Ji sitting at centre facing camera, Ajit to his right and slightly behind, Janak Puri (with hat), and friends. 1946

Travelling between Sirsa and Sikanderpur. *L-R:* Ram Kishan, Lakhi Dharmani, Maharaj Ji, Sohan Singh Bhandari, Harmohinder. Mid '40s

*I*t was in the summer, and it was very, very hot. I had just come from the courts to see the Great Master, who was supervising the work in the sugar cane fields, and he said, "You supervise the work so they don't become slack."

It was so hot, I went into the shade; and being hot, I slept—and the labourers just stopped the work. Great Master came to know, and he asked somebody who told him that I was sleeping. He then came all the way to the fields and, finding me napping, he used his stick. Naturally, I was very alert after that!

I think it was my privilege. He wouldn't use his stick so easily on just anybody. In the evening, Bhai Shadi, who was very close to him and his constant attendant—in the evening we used to massage Great Master's legs and I was doing that as usual—Bhai Shadi said, "Maharaj Ji, you unnecessarily scolded him. He must be very tired in the summer heat and he's not used to all this." Great Master just smiled. He said, "It was best for him. I did it for his betterment." Naturally, I never said anything, neither did I feel bad about it.

Then Great Master himself asked me, "How do you get to the courts?"

I said, "In a tonga. I use the horse."

He said, "It's so hot. Why don't you buy a new car?"

I was quiet. Then he called Lala Munshi Ram and asked him to write a letter to somebody in Delhi to buy me a Hillman car. And the next day I was on my way to Delhi to buy a new car. If he had given me two sticks, God knows what I would have got. My family members were very envious. They all wanted to be in my position!

With Harjeet.

With his cousin Tej (Mrs Garcha) and her friend.

Returning from satsang in Jhelum. Maharaj Ji at the wheel, Rao Sahib beside him, R. C. Mehta standing, S. S. Bhandari and R. N. Mehta seated in the back. 1945

Opposite: In Murree (now in Pakistan). 1945

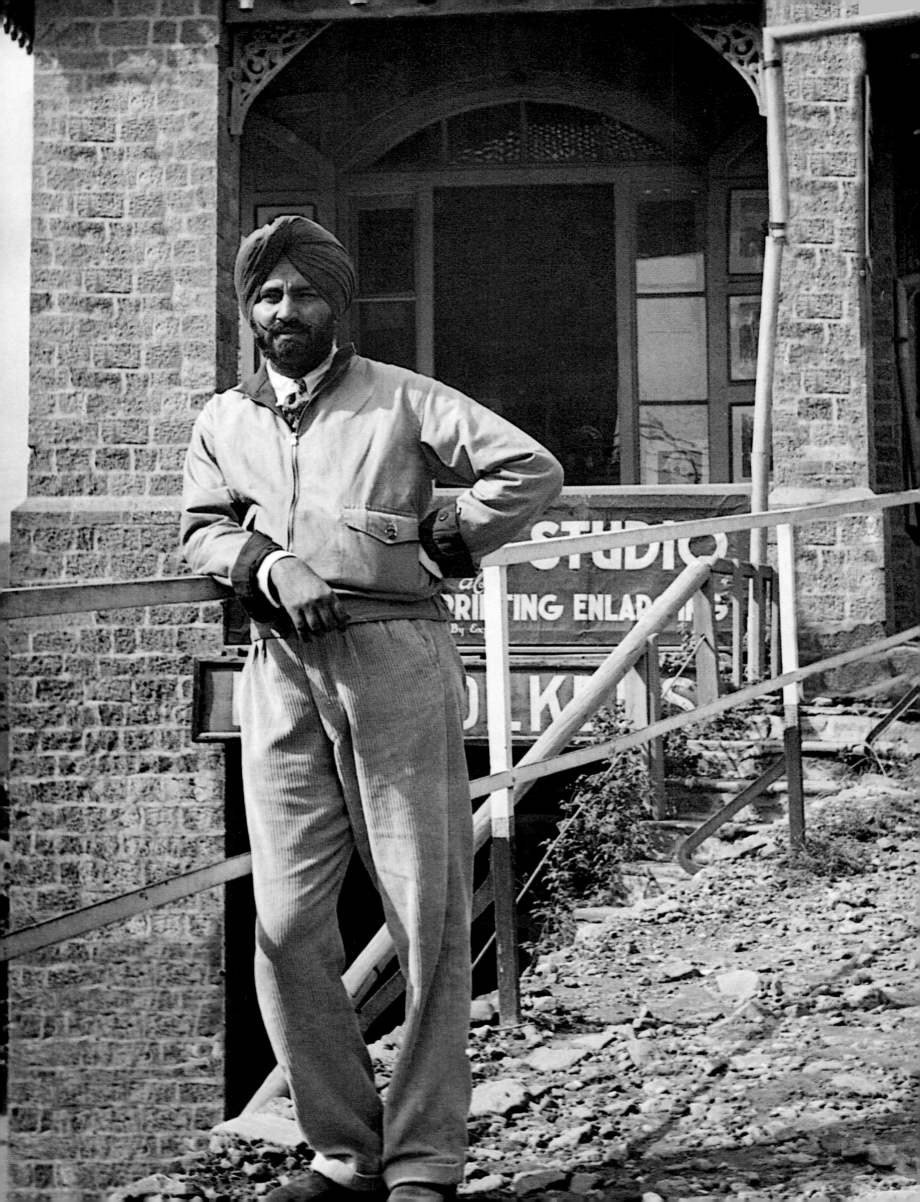

With Nimmi, his first child. 1947

With the family in Sikanderpur. *L-R:* Mohinder, Shoti's wife Satwant, his mother Beji, Gurnam, Maharaj Ji, Satnam holding Nimmi, and Jogi standing in front.

With Cuckoo, his second child.

With his youngest child, Rana. 1951

Celebrating his brother-in-law Ram Kishan's wedding at Pisawa. Maharaj Ji playing harmonium, R. N. Mehta playing *dholak* (drum), Ram Kishan standing (in white coat). 1951

1951

The best plan you can make is to live in His will and accept His commands and be receptive to His grace—that's the best plan we can make. The Lord will make you work, he will create certain desires in you to work—it is not in your hands not to work then. That is also in his hands, to make you work. Everything is in his hands.

CHAPTER TWO
Succession

The *dastarbandi* (tying of the turban) ceremony. Dera, November 4, 1951

*M*y love for Hazur Maharaj Ji, the commands of Sardar Bahadur Maharaj Ji, and the affection of the sangat compel me to carry out the wishes of Sardar Bahadur Ji to serve the sangat and the Dera. But when I look at myself and my shortcomings, I feel diffident and find myself unable to decide whether I am really fit for these onerous duties. This struggle has prevented me so far from meeting the sangat, for which I seek your forgiveness.

I wish to tell the sangat quite frankly that I do not make any claims whatsoever to spiritual attainments. I do not find in myself even those excellences that a good satsangi should possess.

I had the good fortune of being at the feet of Hazur Maharaj Ji and of serving him during the last days of his illness, but Sardar Bahadur Ji did not afford me even this privilege. I am so unlucky that I reached here only after his cremation and could not even have his last darshan.

These orders were communicated to me by those fortunate devoted satsangis who were near Sardar Bahadur Ji, and I have no choice but to serve the Dera and the sangat according to his orders. I request the sangat to look upon me as their younger brother and thus help me in serving them and this great institution. If the sangat looks upon me in any other light, it would mean that you do not wish to support and cooperate with me, and that would be doing a great injustice to me.

The passing away of Sardar Bahadur Ji has been a great shock to all of us. We had not yet got over the grief and sorrow caused by Hazur Maharaj Ji's departure when Sardar Bahadur Ji has also left us. Such personalities rarely come into this world. Only a great and highly advanced soul could lead such an immaculate, spotless life, free from all personal motives. We should not become dispirited nor feel helpless in this hour of our calamity, but should try to follow with confidence and firmness the path of Surat Shabd Yoga pointed out to us by Hazur Maharaj Ji and Sardar Bahadur Ji. Hazur Maharaj Ji used to say that he is always with everyone. This assurance stands for all of us and not for me alone. I request all devoted sevadars of the Dera to faithfully carry out whatever duties he had entrusted to them.

The sangat has assembled from far and near to do homage and pay their respects to Sardar Bahadur Maharaj Ji, and for this I thank you with all my heart.

I repeat today before the entire sangat what I said yesterday to a group of devoted satsangis whom I had called for the purpose, namely, that I do not consider myself worthy of putting on the turban of such great saints. But, compelled by the sangat's love and faith in Hazur Maharaj Ji, I have submitted myself to the sangat, and the sangat can do as they see fit.

43

The true living Master is such a great mystery, the mind can scarcely comprehend it. If, for one's entire life, one were to contemplate this key to God's plan of redemption, one would be fortunate to penetrate even the surface of this mystery.

How can God take an unsuspecting human being and transform him into a saint? How can a mortal being be infused with the power to connect other human beings to the Shabd, that power which sustains the creation? How can a person be empowered to take others back to their Father's home from which they came aeons and aeons ago?

Reading the *dastarbandi* speeches of the Beas Masters, one is struck by the fact that they found themselves absolutely unworthy for the onerous task they were so suddenly and unexpectedly asked to perform. Each accepted the order only because his Master so ordained. For each the bedrock of his life was unconditional obedience to his Master's will. How many times did Maharaj Ji say in so many different ways that he would rather be a devotee, but he had no choice in the matter.

"You get many things even when you don't desire them," he said. "I'm only doing that duty allotted to me by my predecessor. If it were in my hands I would not stay, even for one second, on this stage."

Yet the record of his brilliant mastership stands witness to the perfection of the order. However human he may have felt himself to be, it is the firm conviction of those who knew him that he was an example beyond compare of sainthood, and that when you looked at him, you saw the Lord through him. In his unending graciousness, he brought the qualities of God to earth to share with all.

~

When the youthful, thirty-five-year-old Sardar Charan Singh was appointed by Sardar Bahadur Ji to the Beas *gaddi,* he assumed responsibility for the care of an already large, establshed sangat and became caretaker of the colony of Dera Baba Jaimal Singh, Beas, along with a number of satsang centres and properties scattered around the country.

The preceding few years had been troubled times for the sangat. India had become independent after years of colonial rule. Thousands of people, including many of the sangat, had been uprooted from their homes in Punjab, as Pakistan was carved out of the subcontinent. Great Master, after being Master for forty-five years—during which time the sangat had grown steadily around his magnetic personality—had left his mortal coil and many of his disciples were inconsolable. And Sardar Bahadur Ji's indifferent health during the three years of his mastership had made it impractical for him to restructure the administration of the colony to meet the needs of the expanding sangat and the changing times.

To add to these difficulties, Maharaj Ji had grown up at the Dera, and many of the older satsangis found it difficult to think of him as other than their junior, a young man from Great Master's family, someone who, by their reckoning, had much to learn.

Yet from his earliest days in office, Maharaj Ji's actions were coloured by those qualities that were to distinguish his forty years as Master. As he graciously assumed the central functions of his role—presenting himself before the sangat as their new Master, giving satsang, and then giving Nam, he consistently revealed his greatness through his humility. Whatever he did, he allowed no credit to rest with him, for he had submitted his being to his Master. Never did he miss an opportunity to recall him: his thoughts, deeds, his very breath— all were attributed to him. The more he protested his unworthiness, the more the sangat accepted and loved him. Always considerate of the sentiments of the older generation who had served in the Dera before him, he both strengthened the spirit of harmony and fellowship amongst the sangat while effecting radical changes in the administration. And as he gradually made changes that would carry the organization smoothly into a fast-changing, modern world, he demonstrated his far-reaching vision and practical understanding of administrative matters. By the end of his first decade in office, he had laid a sound foundation for the enormous growth that would take place in the years to come.

The day after the formal installation (*dastarbandi*) of Maharaj Ji as Master. *L-R:* Louise Hilger, Rani Lakshmibai Rajwade, Maharaj Ji, Shoti, Prof. Jagmohan Lal. November 5, 1951

"I am not permitted even to shed tears," had been Sardar Bahadur Ji's words to Maharaj Ji when he first saw Sardar Bahadur after the passing of the Great Master. Now, three years later, Maharaj Ji found himself in that very situation. He, as the Master, was responsible for everyone. Because the Master serves as God's earthly mirror, he cannot express the frailties of a human being—though as a human being, he too feels sorrow, pain and the entire gamut of human emotions.

Shortly after becoming the Master.

From a letter dated October 24, 1951 —

... as I am feeling now, facing people with folded hands, eyes full
with tears and sorrow. When I compare my shortcomings with their
faith, devotion and respect—my mind ceases to think and I am
living as if I have no other alternative ... I have been surrounded,
captured and imprisoned.

1952

Prof. Jagmohan Lal had been Maharaj Ji's teacher and guardian during his college days. One day shortly after his appointment, Maharaj Ji requested the professor to come by and help with the foreign mail. Naturally it was difficult for the professor to absorb the implications of his former student's appointment as Guru. Maharaj Ji, being soft-spoken and shy by nature, was reluctant to demonstrate any kind of authority or impose himself on anyone.

So the professor did not take the request very seriously and chose, instead, to remain in meditation. Maharaj Ji requested him again the next day, and again he chose to stay at home. When Maharaj Ji had made a third request, and when yet once again the professor chose to sit for bhajan, he found that the Shabd was "pushing him out", as he described it. However much he wanted to go in, the Shabd, he felt, would not let him. He was being given a message, he realized: he had to accept the new Master.

Address delivered by Maharaj Ji to the sangat at the monthly satsang in November, 1951 —

I have received many letters from satsangis expressing their anguish and distress. I know that we all feel at this time like little children who have been suddenly orphaned, but we should not forget that the protecting hands of Great Master and Sardar Bahadur Maharaj are still over our heads and they are helping and guiding us in every way.

We should, therefore, try our level best to tread the path which they have chalked for us, nor should we forget the assurance repeated so often by Great Master that he would always be with the satsangis.

The instructions left by Sardar Bahadur Maharaj Ji to me and to the devoted sadhus of the Dera shall be carried out to the best of our abilities, but I hope the sangat will take an indulgent view if, due to our difficulties and short-comings, they have to put up with some inconvenience.

I again take this opportunity to repeat the request which I made shortly after the passing of our late Master, Sardar Bahadur Maharaj Ji, and that is to let me serve the sangat as their younger brother. I earnestly request every satsangi ***not to address me as Maharaj Ji,*** as such titles suit only royal personalities like my illustrious predecessors. I am only a humble servant of the sangat.

I feel that I am like a stone idol in a temple. According to their notions of love, some bathe it with cold water, some with hot water, and some deck it in fine clothes; but it is still an idol all the same.

Distributing parshad. Gandhi, the personal attendant to Great Master, Sardar Bahadur Ji and Maharaj Ji, is in the foreground. 1953

At the farm in Sikanderpur with his father (squatting), Gopal Singh Lattha (the postmaster who served for many years as a scribe in the Dera), Prof. Jagmohan Lal (with black hat) and Ram Kishan. 1952

With Dr Pierre Schmidt. 1953

One of his childhood friends described how, as young men, they were like brothers. It was hard, initially, for him to accept that his friend had become the Master. After Maharaj Ji came to the gaddi, whenever he would pass through his hometown, he would visit him. On the first occasion, he was given a sign he could not deny. As Maharaj Ji was leaving, he took his friend's hand in his own. "I felt a shock like an electric current," he said. "All the time in the train, as I returned to the town where I was then posted, I had ringing in my ears. I said to myself: You fool. Make no mistake of it. He is the Master. Don't think he is anyone else."

In the satsang ghar, Dera. 1953

From a letter dated November 7, 1951, Beas —

I had no alternative left but to accept this heavy responsibility. You can well imagine how hard it will be to carry it out. This has created many other complications and I hardly find any clue to them. I have entirely submitted to Him—His will—and will face whatever He has in store for me. But I want to assure you all, and particularly yourself, that I have not changed and will never change and I will be the same to you....

The first official portrait, taken at the behest of the Indore sangat in October 1953 when Maharaj Ji started initiating.

A soldier, once he joins the army, has no reason to refuse. He has no right to refuse. He never asks why. We have taken a certain discipline on ourself and we have to abide by it.

Dera. Satsang beside the library.

With characteristic humility, Maharaj Ji said that when he first became Master he did not find himself prepared to give satsang. His attention had been always on Great Master or Sardar Bahadur during their satsangs rather than on the scriptural text they explained. In fact he had complained to Sardar Bahadur that his satsangs were too short—Sardar Bahadur Ji never allowed them to last more than three quarters of an hour—and this was because, he said, the sangat wanted more darshan. He also said many times how until he was appointed Master, he hadn't read much in the way of scriptural or Sant Mat books. Everything he knew had been learnt from Great Master and Sardar Bahadur Ji in person.

One day he arrived in the Dera unannounced while satsang was going on. It was being held in the old library square, and Maharaj Ji sat down quietly at the back. What he heard disappointed him. Much of the subject matter did not relate to

Satsang at the library.

Darbari, who for many years sang shabds before the satsang, is standing to the left. Manohar, Maharaj Ji's personal attendant, is next to the two pathis.

the text and emphasis was being given to miracles performed by Great Master. When he complained to his personal assistant, Professor Jagmohan Lal, the professor retorted: "If you do not hold satsang, then what else can you expect?" He went on to say: "You are a law graduate and were successful in your profession, and right from childhood have been brought up in this atmosphere. I don't know why it is not possible for you to hold satsang."

Prompted by this incident, Maharaj Ji gave his first satsang, basing it on Tulsi Sahib's verses, "Cleanse the chamber of your heart." Once again, to their great joy, the sangat had the privilege of receiving spoken guidance from a living Master. From that day onwards, Maharaj Ji gave himself without reserve in the Lord's service as he delivered satsang after satsang after satsang for the next forty years.

Satsang. Pathi Bhan Singh is seated to Maharaj Ji's left.

Satsang on the verandah of the satsang ghar. Speaker Gokul Singh sitting to Maharaj Ji's left with two pathis, as was then the practice. 1955

The seed of Nam is planted within every initiate, and it must sprout. We are advised to protect this crop and preserve the sanctity of this treasure. A crop in an open field will certainly grow without protection, but it remains vulnerable and is easily plundered. We must, therefore, surround our crop which we grow through meditation with the fence of satsang—the company of the Masters and saints and their devotees. Satsang provides an impregnable shield against robbers and thieves who may wish to have us squander that spiritual wealth.

Selection for initiation.

Starting Initiations

The anniversary of Sardar Bahadur Maharaj Ji's passing was commemorated at a bhandara on Sunday, October 25, 1953, with an unusually large number of people in attendance. After Maharaj Ji's forceful, one-and-a-half-hour discourse, Babu Gulab Singh, a highly venerated satsangi of Baba Ji Maharaj's, rose and asked permission to speak. He said: "Several times I have begged Maharaj Ji to start giving initiation to the many souls thirsting for Nam. The entire sangat is eagerly awaiting that great day. The last time I was in Delhi, some devoted satsangis and seekers pressed me to appeal to you to begin initiations. Once again, Maharaj Ji, on behalf of the sangat and seekers, I humbly and respectfully implore you to open your treasure house and begin to bless seekers with initiation."

Babu Gulab Singh's words touched all of us deeply, especially the seekers, who were overjoyed to hear their feelings expressed so clearly. In the silence that followed, the atmosphere was heavy with anticipation. Finally, Maharaj Ji took the microphone and said:

"As Babu Ji has said, he and other satsangis have been urging me to start giving Nam. Hazur Sardar Bahadur Ji also left instructions to that effect. I am a slave of the Master and his sangat …" Then, his voice choked with emotion, Maharaj Ji paused for a few moments. With tears in his eyes he tried again to speak, but overpowered by his feelings, he turned away and left.

The next day, October 26, 1953, Hazur Maharaj Charan Singh Ji opened the floodgates of his grace and mercy and began to give initiation. At 9:00 a.m. he left his house, wearing the shawl that Sardar Bahadur Maharaj Ji had given him, and went into Baba Ji's room in the Great Master's house before proceeding to the Satsang Hall to initiate the seekers. The sangat stood on each side of the road waiting to have his darshan. When Maharaj Ji emerged from the Great Master's house, his face literally seemed to shine with radiance. He proceeded to the Satsang Hall and gave initiation to the seekers there. Initiations abroad, which had been suspended after Sardar Bahadur Ji's departure, were also resumed.

From an account by Daryai Lal Kapur

Meeting with sevadars.

How difficult it is to hear the Master's words! The fact is, we do
not see things as they are. Rather, we see things as we are.

Giving parshad.

To the disciple who was overly respectful, the Sufi Master said, "Light is reflected on a wall. Why venerate the wall? Be attentive to the light."

61

Dera langar.

When Maharaj Ji took over the administration in the early fifties, it was clear that the sangat had already outgrown several of the Dera facilities. The langar had been built to feed just a few hundred people at a sitting, whereas the crowds at bhandara times were already in the thousands. On such occasions people had no choice but to wait until late at night, sometimes even beyond midnight, to eat their evening meal. When Maharaj Ji realized this, he called a meeting with his staff to discuss what changes could be made.

The langar was surrounded on three sides by Dera buildings, so the only possibility for expansion was towards the east where the boundary was marked by the edge of an earlier course of the Beas River. Since Baba Jaimal Singh Ji had first settled there in the previous century, the river had meandered away to the east, away from the small colony, leaving an irregular lattice of deep clay and sand gullies and steep ravines leading down to vast tracts of marshy land. Under Indian law, any such terrain which originally formed part of a river and then becomes exposed may be used by the local community.

Maharaj Ji, to the concern of his advisors, decided these ravines should be filled and levelled. He projected that the need was to feed twenty thousand people at a sitting so that even a crowd of a hundred thousand could be fed within a period of some three hours. It would clearly be a herculean task, and his staff advised him against it. They believed that first of all, the plan was not viable, and even if they attempted such an ambitious task, it would take many years.

Having grown up at the feet of Great Master, Maharaj Ji had already seen what could be done through the power of love. It is said that love can move mountains and Maharaj Ji had himself participated in the construction of the satsang ghar through seva in the thirties.

Now he expanded the langar out of that same love. He announced after satsang that the ravines would be filled as a form of seva. A specific time of day was allocated—once in the morning and once in the evening—and Master himself was present at the site for both periods. It was the beginning of a phenomenon: *mitti ki seva*. This 'service of carrying earth' would continue uninterrupted over several decades. Through it, the sangat would lay the foundations for the growth of the colony, a foundation not just of sandy soil but of such love and joy that it can have few parallels in the world. For the next thirty years, day after day, month after month, mitti seva took place in Maharaj Ji's presence. Hundreds, sometimes thousands, of people would move earth in baskets on their heads to where it was needed. Large hillocks would disappear in a matter of days. Deep ravines would be transformed to level land. This seva was for everyone. Young and old, rich and poor, the able and the infirm, disciples from all over India and from all over the world, everyone could join together in this effort—even if it was to carry just a cupful of sand, if one could not manage more. It brought the sangat together like no other activity could, working shoulder to shoulder, children of one Father, under the ever-present, benign and watchful eye of Hazur. And within two years from when Maharaja Ji first started next to the langar, contrary to the expectations of his advisors, the needed expansion was complete.

Visit of Partap Singh Kairon, the Chief Minister of Punjab, to the Dera.

$\mathcal{W}$e have to keep a balance in life. We can't become recluses—we are part of a chain in this society and you can't break the chain. You can't run away from your responsibilities and obligations and hide yourself in some cave in a forest. You have to discharge certain responsibilities and duties in life. You have karmic accounts to pay, to give and take, that you have to discharge; and while doing that, you also do your meditation. You have to keep the balance.

In the early years, Maharaj Ji used to supervise the entire administration—meetings, correspondence, interviews, and so forth—from the verandah adjacent to the two small rooms that served as the Dera office.

Once, speaking of his responsibilities as Master, he commented that while giving satsang was something he enjoyed, receiving donations on behalf of the institution was for him an ordeal. His entire life he had learnt to give, not to take. This had been his lesson from his supreme mentor, the Great Master who, from his own earnings, had largely provided for the first buildings in the Dera.

Late 1950s.

THE FIRST BOARD OF TRUSTEES, APRIL 2, 1958—RADHA SOAMI SATSANG BEAS

L-R, Front row: Rai Sahib Munshi Ram, Lakshmibai Rajwade of Sangli, Maharaj Charan Singh (Patron), Mrs Parkashwati Sud, Prof. Jagmohan Lal. *Middle row:* Sumeshwar Sahai Bhargava, R. D. Ahluwalia, Lila Ram Daswani, Rai Bahadur Shankar Dass, Tara Chand Aggarwal, Babu Gulab Singh. *Back row:* Damodar Das, Rao Sahib Shiv Dhyan Singh, K. L. Bhargava, E. R. Naidu, Jaswant Singh Claire.

To appreciate how radical Maharaj Ji's decision was to transfer the ownership of all properties and assets to a registered charitable society, one needs to consider it in the context of the preceding half-century.

When Baba Jaimal Singh first settled near the river Beas, he built himself a simple mud hut not far from the river bank in an area of inhospitable wilderness. Naturally, as disciples gathered around him, facilities were needed and gradually a small colony began to take shape in the name of the Master. The Master, personally, owned everything, though Great Master in his last years made a clear distinction between his *parmarthi* (spiritual) and personal properties.

By the time Maharaj Ji was appointed, the colony had grown, and many buildings and lands outside the Dera had been purchased or given to the Master as donations. Maharaj Ji had the foresight to see that an arrangement of private ownership would not serve the sangat well in the future. India was an emerging republic, and land and property laws were being changed to achieve more equitable distribution. This, he saw, would

have direct bearing on the management of sangat affairs and specifically on questions of ownership.

In 1957, Maharaj Ji informed his key sevadars that he wished all Dera assets to be shifted from the Master's name to a trust. His advisors were strongly opposed to the suggestion, saying that it would undermine the basic relationship of disciple and Master.

It was at this time that Rai Sahib Tara Chand Aggarwal, a senior civil servant in the finance department of the Indian government, was initiated. He could see the timely wisdom of Maharaj Ji's suggestion, and from his vantage point, he was also able to convince Maharaj Ji's staff of its need.

With Rai Sahib's help and with his own training and experience as a lawyer, Maharaj Ji then framed the constitution and rules and regulations for the Radha Soami Satsang Beas Society. From then on, all donations would be received by the Trust. The Trust would function entirely for the benefit of the sangat with the Satguru as its Patron, so from the disciple's perspective there was no practical change.

DEED OF TRANSFER

Whereas I, S. Charan Singh Grewal, s/o S. Harbans Singh Grewal, Jat Sikh resident of Dera Baba Jaimal Singh Tehsil and district Amritsar, am a sole trustee by virtue of the registered trust deed dated 24.X.1957 of the properties described in the attached list and the aims and objects of the trust are the same as those of the registered Society named Radha Swami Satsang Beas.

And whereas the aforesaid registered Society lacks funds, property or income requisite to fulfil those aims and objects and I am desirous that the aims and objects of the trust should be pursued and carried out with undivided attention

Now, therefore, I hereby transfer all these properties mentioned in the attached list and of which I am the sole trustee, in favour of the above mentioned Religious and Charitable Society as a trustee.

The Society shall, as a trustee, use, spend and utilize all these properties and their income as well as any other property or properties which I may transfer to it from time to time and any property which the said Society may require, with my consent, hereafter from any source whatsoever, in the advancement, fulfillment and carrying out of these objects and purposes. The Society shall have the same rights and powers and authority as is vested in it by its Rules and Regulations.

With Louise Hilger and Dr Stone.

Meeting with senior sevadars in his garden.

With Mrs Fripp and Peter Fripp (on Maharaj Ji's right).

73

Screening candidates for initiation inside the satsang ghar. Seth Sedhumal Ji, who assisted Maharaj Ji at initiations for many years, is on the extreme left of picture. The lady sevadar in spectacles facing the camera is Dhanoo, who looked after Great Master's house.

Master of Masters! Listen to my plaint:
Whom else shall I address?
To me there is no other like you;
To you there are millions like me.
Read not my scroll of evil deeds,
Shut not your door on this wretched soul.
Had I not been steeped in sin, says Bahu,
On whom would you have showered your mercy?

Sun fariaad peeraan diaa peeraa,
aakh sunaavaan kainoon hoo
Tain jehaa mainoon hor na koee,
main jeheeaan lakkh tainoon hoo
Phol na kaaghaz badeeaan waale,
dar ton dhakk na mainoon hoo
Main wich aid gunaah na hunde,
toon bakhshendon kainoon hoo

Sultan Bahu

Early initiation of overseas visitors at the in Great Master's house.

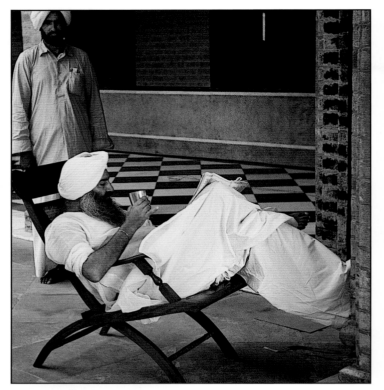

Taking tea during the initiation break.

Attending to mail in the winter sunshine.

Blessing parshad

76

About the best time of life for spiritual practice —

*W*e always try to give the time we have no use for to the Father. Once we are rejected by society, by our children or friends, then we want to devote our time to the Father. When we become old and our senses don't go with us, our eyes refuse to cooperate, ears and limbs refuse to cooperate—then we want to worship the Father. We have to give the best time of our life to the Father.

78

*Y*ou don't fall in love with the Master; Master has fallen in love with us. And then, we become restless—we feel we have fallen in love with him. The pull is from within.

1955

Charan Singh
25/12/55

1964

Soft and tender are saints,
no one else in the world is like them.
There is no one else like them;
they are kind and merciful to all.
Foe and friend are alike to them,
and alike are bad luck and good fortune.
They are as tender as flowers;
not even in a dream do they see others' faults.
They ever wish well to others,
for they savour the wine of divine love.
Affable to all, with a gentle smile,
soft and sweet of speech are they.
Cheerful whatever happens, they emanate coolness;
in every glance they radiate compassion.
Whatever one might say to them,
O Paltu, they are not in the least perturbed.
Soft and tender are saints,
no one else in the world is like them.

Paltu

We have a wrong concept: that our heart should not be soft. It should be very, very soft. Even for our enemies in misery—there should be tears in our eyes.

CHAPTER THREE

Satsang Tours

In March 1952, some four months after becoming the Master, Maharaj Ji gave his first satsang outside the Dera, in Amritsar. A few months later he gave satsang in Kashmir where his family was staying to escape the heat of the plains. Then, in November 1953, he held a satsang programme in Delhi and from there, went on to Agra to make his first official visit to the Dayal Bagh and Soami Bagh centres as the newly appointed Master in Beas.

It was in November 1955, however, that Maharaj Ji made his first extensive tour through India, a tour that was to set the pattern for the next five or six years. These were exhaustive tours that took him from town to town and city to city as he travelled continuously for five to six weeks to spread the teachings of the saints. In some places, such as Delhi or Bombay, there was already a sangat of several thousands, while in others, the teachings were hardly known.

When he travelled by train for these earliest tours, he normally went by second class, using the standard four-berth compartment and often travelling by night so he could give satsang and meet the sangat and seekers during the day. When he went by road, he would often stop to give unscheduled satsangs or darshan where there were even a handful of satsangis in the smaller towns or villages en route. Night after night he would sleep in a different bed, and from November to March he would be away from the Dera for the greater part of the time.

On that first tour, he started by holding satsangs in the northern state of Uttar Pradesh, in Saharanpur, Dehra Dun, Kanpur, Lucknow, Pisawa and Delhi. This was then followed by a tour of central and western India that included Bombay, Indore, and Gwalior. From Bombay he also conducted satsang programmes in nearby Kalyan and Chembur and then proceeded to the royal state of Sangli, where he was a guest of the former Raja. From Sangli he went to the Madhya Pradesh cities of Indore and Ratlam, and while he was based in Indore, he also held a satsang programme in Dewas and the neighbouring village of Devli. This was a village where Great Master had given satsang fifteen years earlier, and where he had promised the people he would return to give satsang again. Now, fifteen years to the day, on the December 15, 1955, Maharaj Ji fulfilled that promise. After Indore he drove to Gwalior, giving satsang in Ujjain and Shivpuri and darshan in the villages of Kanasia and Bilawali en route. Since, on that first tour, he had not begun to initiate, it wasn't until the following year, in response to the many requests from seekers in the towns he visited, that he gave both satsang and initiation wherever he went.

In the early sixties Maharaj Ji decided to change his approach to touring within the country. As a result of his extensive travels, the teachings were spreading and the sangat was growing rapidly. Now, rather than giving one or two satsangs in many different locations, he decided to choose one or two main centres in each state where he would spend several days. People could come from the nearby villages and towns and he would give both satsang and initiation. Accordingly, specific cities, towns and in some cases villages were designated as satsang centres. Initially, this included Delhi, Jaipur, Ajmer and Sikanderpur (Sirsa) in the north, Bombay in the west, Madras in the south, Calcutta and Tatanagar in the east, and Nagpur, Indore, Sangli and Sidhpur in central India.

In many towns, plots of land were purchased and the local sangat came together in seva to build for themselves facilities so that satsang could be held comfortably throughout the year, irrespective of the seasons. At most centres this meant constructing basic amenities such as storage sheds for tenting and other equipment, water tanks, pipelines and bathrooms and, in time, permanent satsang halls that could also be used for initiations.

Throughout his first two decades as Master, Maharaj Ji went regularly to the mountains for part of the summer. Though ostensibly he went to the hill stations of Srinagar, Dalhousie or Mussoorie to relax for some weeks with his family and friends, he would give satsang every Sunday. By the seventies, his schedule no longer allowed for these longer periods of relaxation, but he continued to visit the hills for satsang. Great Master had travelled extensively in the region and Maharaj Ji continued his work through his regular satsang visits to the towns of Bhota, Paror, Kalu-ki-Bar and Mandi and many unscheduled visits to other small towns and villages in the area.

The pattern of visiting major centres throughout the country once or twice a year continued till the early eighties. By this time the sangat had grown so much in many places that the plots of land developed in the sixties and seventies were no longer big enough to hold Maharaj Ji's satsangs. In the major metropolis centres like Delhi and Bombay, larger plots were purchased away from the centre of town. For his annual visits to regional centres, land was rented, but even this proved increasingly difficult, with the continuing growth in India's population paralleled by rapid urbanization.

Then, in 1984, political unrest made it necessary to reappraise Maharaj Ji's tour programmes. With the troubles in Punjab, his satsang programmes outside the Dera were curtailed. Foreigners were banned by the government of India from entering Punjab, so special facilities were created for them in Delhi and Bombay. For the next four years, Maharaj Ji would stay in Delhi for three ten-day sessions, and Bombay for a one-week session each year to hold special meetings and interviews for the Western sangat. Though his overseas tours ceased at this point, he continued throughout the eighties to visit regional centres in India.

SATSANG TOURS IN INDIA

Arriving in Bombay by train. 1964

At Dayal Bagh, Agra. *L-R:* Ram Kishan Singh, R. D. Ahluwalia, Capt. Purshotam Singh, Daryai Lal Kapur, Prof. Jagmohan Lal, Rao Sahib Shiv Dhyan Singh, Maharaj Ji, S. S. Bhargava. 1953

At the Taj Mahal, Agra. 1953

At Dayal Bagh. *L-R:* Shri Sukhya (secretary to H. H. Mehta Sahib), Shri S. S. Bhargava, not known, Rai Sahib Munshi Ram, Rao Sahib, H. H. Mehta Sahib, R. D. Ahluwalia, Maharaj Ji, Shoti, Daryai Lal Kapur, R. N. Mehta, Bhai Bhan Singh. 1953

Satsang. 1955

*W*e have to be receptive to receive His grace. There is no dearth of His grace within, but we are not receptive to it. Our mind is scattered into the whole creation. So we have to withdraw our mind back to the eye centre—put the cup in the right position before it can be filled.

91

Leaving by train. 1955

Speaking some years later of his satsang tours —

I tour all through India. I go to so many centres just to give an opportunity to the local people to meet me. Nothing else. Otherwise, they hear my tapes, they read the same satsangs, and I've nothing new to say every time. It's only a few—three or four—things that I repeat practically every day and that you all hear every day. It's the same thing. But it creates an opportunity of going to the far and distant lands just to be nearer to them, close to them, to meet them, to know them in their own environment.

Arriving in Bombay station. 1956

Arriving at the site of the new satsang ghar at Bandra. Shoti is behind him to the left, Mr Krishin Babani to the right. 1956

With the Bombay sevadars. 1956

From a letter to a friend, written in 1957 —

I do not know where my destiny is leading me. I feel quite a misfit everywhere. Nature always brutally attacks me without the least preparing me for the situation. When I look at my past and present, I always feel—how could I—how can I pass through all this. I actually feel that I am just an actor and simply playing the part. I wonder when it will finish.

1957

At the airport. 1957

Departure from Bombay with his daughter Nimmi and niece Laddi. 1957

*S*ant Mat is not only meditation— it is a way of life. We have to mold ourself in that way of life where we are always with our Master in all the activities of our life. We don't forget him at anytime, anywhere.

With Mr Babani, reviewing plans for the Bombay satsang ghar. 1958

In truth everything and everyone
is a shadow of the Beloved,
and our seeking is His seeking
and our words are His words...
We search for Him here and there,
while looking right at Him.
Sitting by His side, we ask:
"O Beloved, where is the Beloved?"

Rumi

On a boat in Bombay harbour. *L-R:* Lila Ram Daswani, Maharaj Ji, Mr E. R. Naidu, Cdr Y. P. Kapoor. 1959

At the airport. 1959

At the book stall. 1959

Maharaj Ji always stressed the importance
of spiritual practice compared with an in-
tellectual understanding of the scriptures.
Still, he would encourage the sangat to use
books in the right way, so that by reading,
satsang and seva, a fence could be built
around the real crop of meditation. "What
is there to write?" he would say. "What is
there to say? There is only one God. And
we have to go back to him."

1960

103

*R*eal prayer is not by the lips, not by set words. It comes from the heart, and the heart knows the eloquence of silence. The real prayer is surrender to His will.

Above and below: Blessing and distributing parshad. 1961

106

Darshan. 1968

*D*arshan is the helplessness of a disciple looking at his Master. It's a state of a lover looking at the beloved. He never calculates—he doesn't bother what he's gaining or what he's losing. He's so absorbed with the love that he has no time to think. A lover never thinks what he's gaining or what he's losing: he's happy in his love. That is darshan.

1961

1962

Arriving in Bombay from travels overseas.

Speaking twenty years later of the effect of these early tours —

A spider weaves its own net, then it finds itself a prisoner of that net. That is what's happening. Initially, I started touring, giving long tours, going to far off places, just to hold people there that they may not have to come to the Dera. But the effect has been just the reverse. It's always from those centres where I hold satsang that the most people come.

1964

With their hearts in heaven and their feet on earth, the living Masters have a wonderful and characteristic sense of humour. Maharaj Ji once recounted with great enjoyment how in the early days of his satsang tours he had been travelling by car with only his pathi when the car broke down. He was not in the habit of carrying any money with him, and nor did his pathi have any money. To reach the satsang venue on time, they were obliged to hail a bus and so they explained to the conductor they would pay him at their destination. When they arrived, however, there right before everybody was the huge shamiana and all the arrangements for satsang. They had to enter, so to speak, from the bus and organize the fare!

1964

1966

1972

His voice was gentle, melodious and soothing; in fact, as you listened to him, it seemed to flow like honey. One recalls the murmur of anticipation and excitement that always swept through the sangat each time he began to speak, for they loved to hear his voice. Satsang would last for up to two hours, during which he would speak for long periods without a break, without a sip of water, no matter what the weather—the cold of winter or the heat and dust of the summer.

1972

1986

114

1987

Arriving for the English meetings with Westerners. 1987

*W*hen you love somebody, you always like to gaze at his face. When you are so pulled by that face, you develop your love, strengthen your love. You help your love to grow; it grows automatically. That is darshan.

With Raja Sahib Sangli and Shoti.

Leaving Bombay by the Deccan Queen, we arrived at the Miraj railway station via Poona on 9 December at 1:00 p.m. Raja Sahib had been waiting at the Miraj station since four in the morning, but our train was running nearly seven hours late, due to a line block on the way. Subsequently, we were all comfortably lodged in Raja Sahib's palace.

The satsang at Sangli starts at 5:00 p.m. in the old palace of the Raja Sahib. At the end of Maharaj Ji's satsang, the discourse is translated by a satsangi into the Marathi language for the benefit of the gathering. This gentleman is a retired Deputy Postmaster General, and he also records on tape the satsangs of Maharaj Ji.

Raja Sahib took us around his gardens, some of which have very tall coconut trees. The people of this area are highly cultured, most unassuming and quiet.

From an account by Rai Sahib Munshi Ram Ji, Maharaj Ji's secretary

Lunch at the palace with the Raja Sahib's family members. 1955

*S*implicity doesn't mean to live in misery and poverty. You have what you need, and you don't want to have what you don't need.

117

Seated: Raja Sahib Sangli, Maharaj Ji. *Standing, L-R:* Rao Sahib (Maharaj Ji's father-in-law), Dr Stone, Shoti. 1958

With Rao Sahib and Shoti.

Satsang. 1964

Back row: Visitors from overseas travelling with Maharaj Ji, with palace attendants at both ends. *Seated, L-R:* R. D. Ahluwalia, Rajkumar of Sangli (the Raja's son), the Rani and Raja Sahib on either side of Maharaj Ji, Bibi Ralli, Nimmi. *Front row:* Cuckoo and Rana. 1964

Leaving by train with Mr Ahluwalia.

In a letter written to a friend in the late fifties, Maharaj Ji gave some hint of the demanding nature of his travels:

You will find from my programme that at night I am in the train and during the day I have to hold two satsangs. If you just care to place before you the railway map, you will just know as to what I am going through. Now I know with what difficulties and from what distances people come to Beas. Their eyes are full of tears of love and affection. How I wish that I be worthy of all that they show and do for me.

1955

A conviction based on public miracles is shallow and short-lived. We should be so absorbed in love and devotion for the Father that external evidence has no influence on our faith.

With the Sethi family. 1955

1956

With Mr V. K. Sethi.

Exchanging greetings with Mr B. L. Sethi.

Arriving at Indore.

By nature, Maharaj Ji was a shy person and embarrassed by any outward ceremony. But such was his regard and consideration for the feelings of others, especially for his elders, that he would readily forego his own preferences for the sake of others. Thus, in Indore, he would always accept a garland from the elder Mr Sethi as head of the family, on arrival and departure, since this was their custom. He would smilingly and graciously accept the garland, and only after Mr Sethi's death he established his own preference and instructed the family: No more garlands!

Dr Pierre Schmidt, seeing the way Maharaj Ji was not sparing himself, cautioned him in the early sixties that if he didn't reduce his work load and take more rest, he would either develop diabetes or heart trouble. But Maharaj Ji's concern was for the sangat—there was no question of curtailing his schedule—so by the seventies, he had both.

With Dr Pierre Schmidt. 1962

1964

126

At the Holkar palace.

With the Sethi family. 1964

Initiation selection.

Maharaj Ji's tours were extremely taxing. On one occasion in Indore, so as not to have to disappoint anyone, he held three initiation sessions in a day, using petromax lamps for the evening session and taking his dinner finally at 11:00 p.m. He then left for Delhi by train, travelling overnight, to give satsang there the following day. From Delhi, he proceeded to Beas to be there in time for the bhandara. His concern for the sangat was without limits. A decade later, after he had had his first heart attack, he explained to his doctor why there was no question of him cutting back his schedule:

> *Doctor Sahib, when a fisherman throws gram [roasted chick peas] in the water to attract the fish into his net, if the fish gather in large numbers, he does not then refuse to pull the net, saying it is too heavy. This he should have realized when he threw the gram into the water. Now he has no option but to haul in the entire load. Now there is no way but to initiate these souls. Do not worry, I will be all right. Doing Great Master's work never tires me. I am happy to do my duty.*

सत पुरुष की आरसी संतों ही की देह
लगाना चाहे अतस को उन्हें खलह

Satsang. 1957

*A*ctually, Sant Mat is so simple. There's just
a few things we discuss everyday—and it has
its effect. Even a drop falling on a stone makes
its own place there. That is the effect of satsang,
of the group meetings.

Some people being far away may be nearer to the Master than people nearer to him. This 'nearness' and 'far away' doesn't make any difference at all. How much love people have in their heart, that makes them near or far away—it is not the physical nearness which matters.

Nagpur. 1950s

Bangalore. 1963

Satsang in the Glass House, Bangalore. 1981

Ahmedabad. 1963

Talking about his approach to satsang—

Generally I do not narrate any stories in satsang. I start at one speed and finish at the same speed. My approach is more like that of a lawyer, an advocate—I used to practise as one—where you have to convince people on certain points. I am fond of giving a lot of quotations, just as you argue a point in court and give so many high court rulings to corroborate it. So the approach of every mystic is according to his own background and the background of the people to whom he is explaining.

Selecting canditates for initiation in Ahmedabad. 1963

Ahmedabad. 1963   *Opposite:* Baroda. 1960s

From a letter to a friend written on January 20, 1964 —

*Y*ou must have read in the newspapers about the disturbances in Calcutta. Incidentally, I was there during those days on my satsang tour. I was holding satsang at Mohammedan Park, predominated mostly by Muslims, and had one of the most unique experiences of my life on this satsang tour.

While I was holding satsang, shooting, arson, and firing were going on within our sight. Though there was a gathering of about three thousand people, not a single one moved or felt concerned as to what was happening all around. I was myself surprised to witness such faith and love. The satsang went on for a couple of hours, and just after the satsang dispersed, the military took over and put a curfew there. Every satsangi returned home quite safely. None of us were hurt at all.

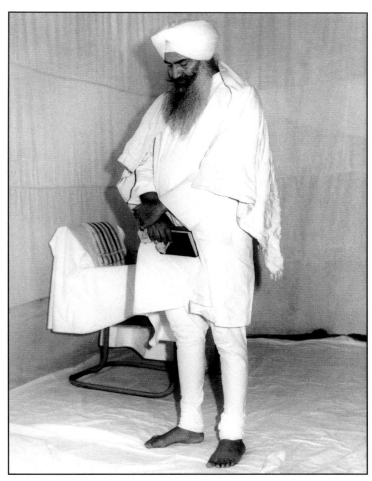

Blessing and distributing parshad. 1964

With Mrs Bharat Ram on his left, Mrs Cami Moss on his right, and Mr and Mrs Lal and their daughter-in-law.

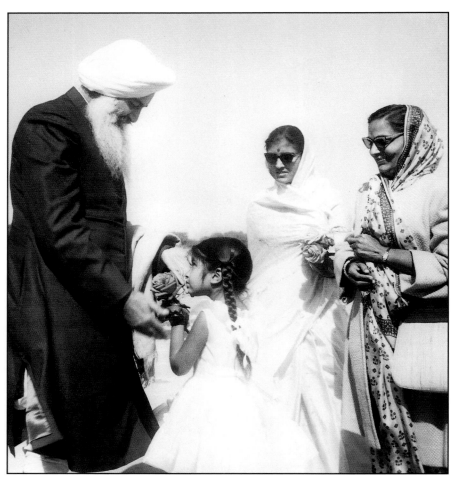

With Mrs Raj Bhalla and Mrs Satwant Narang. Late '60s

With R. N. Mehta (in sunglasses), Mr Bhalla (carrying suitcases) and others. Late '60s

During one of his satsang programmes in Mandi in Himachal Pradesh, there was an interval of two days between the official engagements, which enabled Maharaj Ji to make an overnight trip to Manali, a hill station renowned for its beauty. On leaving the Mandi circuit house in the early morning, Maharaj Ji instructed the driver to turn left—the opposite direction to Manali. His host pointed out the mistake but Maharaj Ji insisted. Again the host, thinking that Maharaj Ji was under some misapprehension about the roads and the route, said that turning left would take them to-wards Pathankot and not Manali. Maharaj Ji insisted.

Not far down the road, they came to the Mandi satsang ghar, where Maharaj Ji immediately got down from the car, climbed the few steps leading into the building, and entered a small room where two sevadars were seated on the floor with their heads bowed, eyes closed. Both men were physically disabled. Both had missed the satsang on the previous day due to the seva they had been given. Now, with all the excitement of the first satsang over, they were experiencing a sense of loss that they, too, had not heard Maharaj Ji's words and had not enjoyed the sweetness of his darshan along with their colleagues. Maharaj Ji stood quietly before them until they opened their eyes. One can well imagine what their state must have been when they realized who was there. After a few moments, he said to his host: "All right, let's go!" And they retraced the road until they reached the turning to Manali.

In a letter written on November 13, 1966, Maharaj Ji commented on Great Master's intensive tours:

I often wonder how Maharaj Ji could reach those places, especially in those days when there were hardly any roads. I am told he often walked for ten to twenty miles, and sometimes rode a horse all day just to reach those spots and stay in those small huts, which are not even well venti-lated, what to say of having an attached bathroom. His efforts are bearing fruit now, as Sant Mat is spreading far and wide in the Himachal area. We have so many beautiful satsang ghars at various places, constructed by Maharaj Ji, which are quite comfortable for me and the sangat.

Above: Maharaj Ji's satsang, early 1960s.
Right: Great Master's satsang at the same location, early 1940s.

Satsang. 1975

And about his own exhaustive tours he wrote:

*N*o doubt my tour in Himachal was very tiring, but it is really a unique experience to see simple hill people coming from such great distances to attend satsang. Sant Mat is spreading like wildfire in the hills. The people are very honest, innocent and sincere, and they easily grasp these simple teachings. Our so-called civilization has not much penetrated into the hills yet, so the people are quite straightforward and honest. It is a sight to see the rolling tears at the time of hearing satsang and their eyes full with love and affection. Yet they do not say a word to express what they feel.

Leaving satsang.

141

Resting on the verandah of the satsang hall. 1975

From a letter to a friend, written on March 21, 1974 —

*B*y His grace I am keeping fairly good health for my age, but my only problem is that I have to travel a lot, and I am always loaded with work. I just move in a circle, where I don't know which is the beginning and which is the end. If I should write my travel programme to you, you would just be shocked, especially what I had to do in the last two months. Anyway, there is nothing to worry about. I get good sleep, and appetite is good, pulse and blood pressure are good, and the heart is still working and active.

1987

1986

English meeting at the satsang ghar, Pusa Road. 1987

Due to instability and terrorism in Punjab, the Indian government did not allow overseas visitors into Punjab from 1984 to 1989. After his trip to South Africa in 1982, Maharaj Ji no longer travelled abroad. With the Punjab closed to foreign passport holders and Maharaj Ji no longer travelling, how could his overseas disciples see him, sit in his presence, have his darshan, hear his satsangs and seek personal guidance when the need arose? In July 1985, Maharaj Ji wrote to all his representatives abroad:

> Our sangat here is incomplete without the presence of our brothers and sisters from abroad and so are my activities. But such is the will of Hazur Maharaj Ji and we live in it. I am eagerly looking forward to the day when we will be able to throw open the gates of the International Guest House to brothers and sisters from abroad. Anyone who wishes to visit Delhi during my stay there will be most welcome. No satsangi should feel disheartened. All are very near to me and I have every one of you in my mind. Do keep attending to simran and bhajan where peace and bliss lie.

With Mr R. N. Mehta. 1987

Interviews during seva. 1989

*T*he greatest miracle of the mystics is that they change the very attitude of our life, the way of our life. They turn everything upside down in our life. That is the greatest miracle the saints come to perform in our lives.

A child has no ego at all. He has no sense of attachment with anything. You give him a small piece of stone, he'll play with that; you give him a diamond, he'll play with that. He's so innocent, you see. Whoever loves him—he belongs to him: he has no ego. We have to become like little children—we have to eliminate our ego. We have to become humble and accept, like the little child, whatever comes our way.

151

At Pusa Road Centre.

Refreshments at Pusa Road Centre.

English meeting at the Chhattarpur farm, Delhi.

*T*o go back to the Father's house is the main purpose of our coming into this life. All other things we do simply to maintain ourselves in this world. But while doing so, we should not forget the Father who has given us all these things.

Visiting the langar at Chhattarpur.

Blessing parshad.

*T*he value of seva is not how much one offers, but
in the feelings and love with which it is offered.

Before satsang.

Darshan at sevadar's parshad.

This longing is something personal. It cannot be broadcast and it cannot be shared with anybody. It is just within every one of us. And even if you try to share it, how can you share it? This is to be digested. This is something which is your personal treasure.

Satsang Tours Abroad

Detroit, U.S.A. 1970

Maharaj Ji's satsang tours abroad were as intensive and extensive as every other aspect of his mastership. When he first began initiating in 1953 there were less than three hundred satsangis outside India. By the time he passed from this world, there was hardly a corner of the globe where practioners of the path of Sant Mat were not to be found—either in the form of a small group of disciples getting together whenever possible for satsang, or as one or two disciples relying on tapes recordings and books for their contact with the teachings, or in the form of established groups of people with their own meeting places and regular satsang programmes.

Though neither Great Master nor Sardar Bahadur Ji had travelled abroad, the message of Surat Shabd Yoga had already spread to distant parts of the world during their lifetime. Naturally, their overseas disciples had longed to see them and requests had come from America in particular that they should grace the sangat with their presence.

As soon as Maharaj Ji began initiating, more and more requests came for him to travel. So, in 1961, almost ten years after he had succeeded Sardar Bahadur Ji, he embarked on his first official foreign tour with a journey to the Far East. Over the next twenty years, every continent had the pleasure of receiving him. The tours mostly lasted between two and three months. Some years he concentrated on a particular area—such as the Far East, Africa, or Europe—while on others, he girdled the globe. In all he made twelve tours, and wherever he went, he planted seeds of spirituality that never ceased to grow.

As in India, his discourses attracted people from all walks of life and all faiths. His universal message of the inner path to God, stripped of all outward rituals, complications and dogma, was heard with rapt attention in auditoriums, gurdwaras, hotel halls and rooms, and private homes in every country he visited. Through the sixties and seventies, there was a spirit of awakening accompanying the increasing prosperity of the industrialized world, a questioning of long-accepted religious values. Disillusioned with their established religious practices, people were drawn by Maharaj Ji's clear, simple message and his radiant presence. His infectious smile, keen sense of humour, affectionate behaviour and above all, his love, generated an atmosphere that dissolved barriers and all formalities. Disciples who had never seen him felt that they had known him for years—that meeting him was simply the renewal of an earlier friendship. In small and large gatherings, he answered questions and resolved confusions with such patience, compassion and clarity that all who heard him were left with no doubt of the truth of his message.

On each tour he would take with him one or two companions, and amidst his hectic schedule, he would always make time for sightseeing and for photography. This he managed in spite of a routine that would keep him busy through a twelve to sixteen hour working day. One of his close associates in Dera commented that with his slide shows, he took his friends with him through the entire world without them having to step beyond the walls of the colony.

He had an extraordinary capacity for hours of sustained effort. Notwithstanding his long hours and the constant changes in time zones, he always looked perfectly fresh and relaxed as he gave satsangs in Punjabi and English, gave darshan and initiations, held numerous private and group interviews, and made himself available to the sangat through receptions, coffee breaks and tea parties so that anyone who wanted to could have an opportunity to meet him personally.

As with every other facet of his mastership, it is impossible to do justice to the magnitude and impact of these tours. By looking at a basic itinerary of the twelve journeys, one has a glimpse of the framework in which he did his work. Pictures and extracts of his words from different tours and different parts of the world act as cameos, capturing a few moments or occasions here and there. Four books—*Light on St Matthew, Light on St John, The Master Answers* and *Thus Saith the Master*—remind us of the talks he gave, for, as with all great teachers, Maharaj Ji built on what his audiences already knew as he referred to some of the best loved scriptures of the West to explain the mystic path. The real legacy of these journeys, however, lies in the hearts of people of all nations, colours and creeds scattered across the face of the globe for whom he opened a dynamic pathway of love to the inner Lord.

THE INTERNATIONAL TOURS

1961 – FAR EAST
Sri Lanka, Burma, Vietnam, Thailand, Singapore, Hong Kong, Philippines, Japan

1962 – MIDDLE EAST AND EUROPE
Iran, Lebanon, Turkey, Switzerland, Germany, France, Sweden, United Kingdom; private visits to Norway, Denmark, Italy and Spain

1964 – AROUND THE WORLD
Thailand, Singapore, Vietnam, Hong Kong, Japan, United States, United Kingdom, Switzerland, Italy

1966 – AFRICA, EUROPE AND MIDDLE EAST
South Africa, Kenya, Tanzania, United Kingdom, Germany, Switzerland, Austria, Israel

1968 – FAR EAST AND OCEANIA
Thailand, Hong Kong, Japan, Singapore, Australia, New Zealand, Fiji

1970 – AROUND THE WORLD
Greece, Switzerland, Netherlands, United Kingdom, Bermuda, West Indies (Barbados, Trinidad, Jamaica), Mexico, United States, Canada, Japan, Hong Kong

1971 – FAR EAST
Philippines, Japan, Thailand, Taiwan, Singapore, Indonesia, Sri Lanka

1975 – MIDDLE EAST AND EUROPE
Iran, Turkey, Greece, Italy, Spain, Canary Islands, Gibraltar, Morocco, Germany, Switzerland, France, Netherlands, United Kingdom

1976 – AROUND THE WORLD
Sri Lanka, Singapore, Australia, New Zealand, Thailand, Japan, United Kingdom, Spain

1979 – EUROPE
Greece, Italy, Switzerland, Germany, Sweden, United Kingdom, Gibraltar, Canary Islands

1980 – FAR EAST
Sri Lanka, Singapore, Indonesia, Thailand, Philippines, Hong Kong, Korea, Japan

1982 – AFRICA
Tanzania, Zimbabwe, South Africa, Kenya, Mauritius

In Saigon with R. N. Mehta. 1961

From a letter written on board ship, June 28, 1961 —

I had been very busy holding satsang everywhere—attending so many receptions. This trip is not a rest in the real sense, rather I am quite exhausted and tired. I am lucky to have a place on this ship. This is another experience I never had before. On the ship you have a world of your own—quite unconcerned with what is happening outside. I travelled quite incognito till Saigon, but there someone brought a newspaper which had my photo, as interviewed by the press. Now everybody is anxious to discuss religion and it is amazing what a poor knowledge people have of their own faith. I think the most wonderful time I have had during this trip is surely the period I am spending on the boat.

With Vietnamese school children and R. N. Mehta, and *(below)* sightseeing in Bien Hoa. 1961

Satsang in the Bangkok gurdwara. 1961

*I*f your boat is caught up in the storm and you find a shore, how relieved you feel. We are all in the storm of our mind and when we go to the satsang of the mystics, we find a shore to land. How relieved we feel. Satsang is a great anchor. We are always influenced by the company we keep.

Satsang. 1968

With Buddhist monks in Bangkok.

Travelling by boat with Bea Jauncey. 1968

Satsang in the Hong Kong gurdwara. 1968

Satsang. 1970

If you want to see in the eyes of the Master, come here to
the eye centre. Then look very deep into his eyes if you can.

With Ken and Cami Moss, overlooking Hong Kong harbour. 1968

When Maharaj Ji spent time with you, inspite of his hectic schedule he made you feel he had nothing else to do but talk to you. He gave you everything. Even a few moments of his time—and one felt one had been with him for an eternity.

Sightseeing by boat and shopping for fabrics.

*I*f so much can be achieved with modern science, what about the divine science? If you can hear BBC here today, across thousands of miles, why can't we hear the Lord's voice within ourselves? When we enjoy so many plays on TV, why can't we enjoy the inner realms within ourselves? It's just a question of tuning the mind.

Satsang. 1961

Satsang. 1968

With Otto, a young satsangi from Germany who was living in Singapore. 1968

With the Melwani family. 1968

Satsang in the Kobe gurdwara. 1968

When we entered the room which serves as the Sikh temple, we found about two dozen people seated on the floor and shabds being sung by a man playing a harmonium, and two other men playing a drum and a tabla. This was about 11:15, and at 11:30 Mr Kishanchand Mahbubani introduced Maharaj Ji, who rose from the floor where he had been sitting and sat on the dais beside the man who had been reading from the Granth Sahib. For an hour and forty minutes Maharaj Ji held everyone in rapt attention, and before long there were about 200 people sitting and standing listening to his discourse all about Sant Mat. From what I could judge, it was a beautiful satsang given specially for all those people who are not satsangis. When we left Osaka all of those who came to see Maharaj Ji away were in tears, and some already want to have Nam. Wherever Maharaj Ji goes people learn to love him and don't want to leave him.

Letter from Bea Jauncey, May 25, 1968

Arrival in Japan. 1968

Ordering tea on the bullet train, and *(below)* travelling on the local train.

Visit to Japan, accompanied by Harjeet and Mr Babani. 1971

*B*ecome a universal citizen! Let us belong to God.

Maharaj Ji's approach to photography was absolutely professional. Like any other work in his daily schedule, he applied himself to it with complete concentration and care. Once behind the camera all else was forgotten, as he went into every little detail—form, texture, composition, light and shade, and the exposure technicalities. In fact, the quality of his work was such that numerous books could easily have been prepared from his work.

Photographing in Kyoto, with Krishin Babani. 1980

*E*verybody wants to be happy in this world—nobody wants to be miserable. So why not be happy? Why not lead a relaxed and happy life? Why should we be all the time worrying about the past, and worrying about the future, and not living with the present at all? You see, relaxation comes only when you're happy within. When you are able to obtain that peace within—then wherever you go, you radiate peace.

At Bali airport. 1968

In Bali, which I thought was too remote for anybody to be there, there were nearly a dozen people to again greet Maharaj Ji. You can imagine what people are really thirsting for, and it is impossible for Maharaj Ji to be able to get away even in the remotest places on earth. Bali was very beautiful, a lot like the Kashmir valley as far as paddy growing goes. There are hills and hot springs and the mighty ocean and plenty of unadulterated air. The people, mostly Hindus, are quite simple in the way they live. Maharaj Ji really enjoyed the island. We left for Jakarta on June 8.

June 9 was the day of the satsang at the gurdwara. Again there were so many that the place overflowed with people. On June 10 Maharaj Ji gave darshan in the morning followed by private interviews for nearly an hour and a half. It was also announced that there would be an initiation on June 12. We have to leave for the airport in a short while. At the moment Maharaj Ji is sitting inside giving darshan to nearly 350 people.

Letter from Madan Mehta, June 23, 1968

Satsang in the gurdwara. 1968

We left for the interior of Java at about 11:00 to visit Bandung and other places. It was a wonderful trip and Maharaj Ji enjoyed every bit of it. The island of Java is as beautiful as Bali, if not more. Here in the interior, people were not so much for tips every time we photographed them as they were in Bali.

Letter from Madan Mehta

Left: Photographing Madan posing with a local farm worker's hat.

Sightseeing in Hamburg, Germany, with Janak Puri, Elsa Svalbe and Naomi Walberg. 1962

At that time, there were only three satsangis in Germany and one was a disciple of Maharaj Sawan Singh, and therefore there was absolutely no need for any kind of satsang arrangements whatsoever. This meant, too, that Maharaj Ji did not have to stick to a tight schedule; in fact, there was no schedule at all.

Letter from Naomi Walberg, 1962

Copenhagen, Denmark. 1962

Hamburg. 1962

Swiss Alps. 1964

Swiss Alps. 1966

On July 6, 1964, Maharaj Ji arrived in Geneva, Switzerland, from England. The handful of German satsangis and seekers at that time had been invited to come to Switzerland. Dr Schmidt had prearranged car and cable trips up the most beautiful parts of the Swiss Alps. Accommodation in the various hotels along the way had been made by him for the whole group, and the best available rooms reserved for Maharaj Ji. At mealtime, we had reserved tables with the vegetarian menus waiting for us. Dr Schmidt being a perfectionist, the arrangements, too, were perfect.

Observing Dr Schmidt's perfect arrangements, Maharaj Ji asked whether he had seen the letter from Dera requesting the sangat to keep everything simple for his visit. Dr Schmidt's reply was yes, he had. But how, he asked, could a diamond be kept in a matchbox!

On this trip, we also cabled up to Mont Blanc in France. One day, going up to one of the awe-inspiring peaks, the sway of the cable car upon takeoff took me completely by surprise. I let out a teeny weeny yell at which Master fumbled in his coat pocket and produced a protein pill (which had been given to him in the States, I believe). He offered it to me, and naturally I did not refuse. "That won't help!" was Dr Schmidt's dry remark, to which Master responded, "Only psychological!"

Naomi Walberg

With *(L-R)* Erich Michalke, Dr Pierre Schmidt, Rudolf and Naomi Walberg in Switzerland. 1964

Swiss Alps. 1966

Roadside picnic while driving from Germany to Switzerland.
L-R: Maharaj Ji, Rudolf and Noami Walberg. 1966

Visiting a cathedral in Freiburg, Germany. 1966

We returned to the Rhine and continued along it to Bonn, the German capital. We stayed in a hotel for the night. The next morning it was lightly drizzling; we wanted to go to the garden show in Bonn. As we pulled off, Maharaj Ji settled down in his seat and remarked, "Ah, fine weather!" "How can you say that? It's wet," we retorted. "It could be pouring," was the optimistic reply and so typical of him throughout the trip. We weren't allowed to say anything negative; he would immediately find something positive about it, which would always result in a burst of happy laughter.

Naomi Walberg

Satsang in Amsterdam, Holland, with Mr Babani and Lionel Metz. 1975

From a letter to a friend, written on August 18, 1975 —

*W*ell, you have been hearing about my hectic satsang tour and I was able to visit practically every satsang centre in Europe. It is very encouraging to find so many people coming to the path and to enrich myself with their love and devotion. Old centres are growing fast and some new centres are coming up. Many books are being translated into their local languages. I must admit it was quite tiring to move from place to place, country to country, packing and unpacking, holding meetings, giving interviews and then rushing out for sightseeing.

Holland. 1970

With Dr T. N. Mathur *(front left)*, Mr and Mrs Zielinski, Rudolf Walberg (centre), Mr Babani (right) in Munich, Germany. 1975

Norway. 1979

With Elsa Svalbe and Janak Puri in Norway. 1979

Malaga Airport. 1975

At the Alhambra Palace. 1979

At Canteras Beach in Las Palmas. 1975

*Y*our Master is within you. He's always watching you, whether
you are conscious about it or not. You can't escape his eyes.

With Elsa Svalbe and Dr Mathur in Morocco.

Morocco

With the Bhojwani family and Dr Mathur in Iran. 1975

Satsang at the Ealing Town Hall. 1962

I have often said that it is a pity that people hate and cut each other's throat in the name of religion, which should rather fill them with love and devotion for the Lord. It is through love, forgiveness and the serving of humanity that one's life becomes a single vision of the sublime beauty of God. Unfortunately, we forget the real teachings of the mystics and unnecessarily arrest them in some rigid organization, thereby giving them the shape of a religion or cult. Religion should make us at least human, if not divine.

Satsang at St. Ermine's Hotel. *L-R:* Sam Busa, Maharaj Ji, Colonel C. W. Sanders and Mrs Bridget Amies. 1962

Tea at Gloucester Place, London. 1962

Visiting Mr and Mrs Forester's home on his way to satsang in Birmingham. 1962

Heathrow Airport. *Seated, L-R:* Mrs Krishna Ahuja, Ron Wood, Mrs F. E. Wood, Maharaj Ji, Mrs Bridget Amies. 1962

Travelling by train from Southampton to Waterloo Station, London, after arriving by ship (the Queen Mary) from America. 1964

Q: Would you please tell us the story again about the man on the ship who sat down at your table with a glass of beer?

A: I can assure you I didn't taste it, though I paid for it. It was the first time I went to the States, you see, and I was booked to go from New York to London by ship. On a ship you generally get acquainted with people— and nobody knew who I was, nor did I tell anybody. I was alone, without any staff member or secretary. Louise had booked me in a first-class cabin and I had it all to myself.

I was sitting in a lounge, probably having a cup of tea, and a gentleman came over with a glass of beer. He knew me just from the deck, not very intimately, just "hello, hello," as you say. He was sitting opposite me and enjoying himself, naturally—and he stayed about fifteen to twenty minutes. Then he was called— perhaps some telephone or his wife was looking for him, he got some message. He left the glass with a little beer in it and walked away. Probably the management waited for him to return, I don't know, or they thought he was with me, so they brought a common bill: a cup of tea and a glass of beer! I kept the bill, but I thought the gentleman would come back. I waited fifteen to twenty minutes aimlessly and I couldn't wait any more. The waiter came twice or thrice to collect the bill. He just looked at me, probably thinking I didn't have any money. Ultimately, I had no alternative, you see. I just paid the bill and went to my room. And perhaps it was early the next morning that the ship landed and I never saw the gentleman after that. I couldn't help it.

194

At Waterloo Station, London, with (on his left) Colonel C. W. Sanders and Gurchetan Singh Johal. 1964

At Heathrow Airport, leaving the U.K. 1964

Speaking at his last official meeting before leaving the U.K. in 1964 —

I can only say a few last words—I have nothing more to give in advice. The books are full of the teachings so I can only suggest that everybody should try to love one another. The more you are nearer to each other, the more you will be nearer and dearer to me. The more we are nearer and dearer to each other, the more we are nearer and dearer to the Lord. We should always try to keep this in our minds. We should, in our group meetings, always be in harmony; there should always be love, affection and understanding. Try to help each other. Try to strengthen each other's faith; try to strengthen each other on the path. That is the real service we can do.

I always advise that our group meetings should be open to everybody—our arms should be open to everybody. We should give a warm welcome to whomsoever wants to come and join us, but for that we must develop love and affection within ourselves. That is the only thing which can impress others, the only thing which can welcome others. If there is no love within ourselves, there is no love within our group meetings, I think we are not coming up to the mark that Sant Mat expects from us. So I can only ask you again, as Christ also taught us, "Love one another."

With Bea Jauncey, Janak Puri, and the Ahuja family. 1970

With Dr and Mrs Garcha.

At Bloomsbury Centre, London, accompanied by Janak Puri, Colonel Sanders and Bob Bear. 1970

A short beautiful song of yearning and love for the Master was sung in English; then Master opened the Bible at the Gospel according to Saint John. All Masters are one; their teachings are one; the Lord is one—and we are to become at one with the Lord. The drop becomes part of the ocean; it is no longer separated. Masters close the door on the world for their initiates, and release them on a journey through many mansions, many regions, until they reach that home which they left as pure souls many aeons ago.

Letter from Colonel C. W. Sanders, May, 1970

London. 1970

Where is room in the imagination for his essence, that the like of him should come into the imagination? How should I—not a vein of mine is sensible—describe that Friend who hath no peer?

Rumi

*I*f you have a kind and loving heart then you are kind and loving to everybody—you are helpful to everybody. You see, if we are filled with love and devotion for the Father, all such qualities rise in us like cream on the milk. You don't have to strive for them—they become part and parcel of you—because then you see the Lord in everyone and you are humble before every one.

Heathrow Airport, London.

200

Arriving at the West Centre Hotel, London. 1979

The programme for the day was a reception to welcome the overseas guests from U.S.A., South Africa and other countries, and to get together with the satsangis and seekers from all parts of U.K. Maharaj Ji was not expected to attend. But somehow Maharaj Ji asked us to get ready to go to the West Centre Hotel. It was a surprise visit. But I believe he wanted to have darshan of his sangat as much as the sangat wanted to have his darshan. Nay, even more. In truth he is the lover. But when he kindles and inspires love in us, we become lovers and think and call him the Beloved. God loves us and therefore comes down in the garb of a human being to take us back to our original home. A Muslim mystic has said, "God is love, God is the lover and God is the Beloved." It is all his play—beyond human understanding. So he entered the hall, joy written on his face, and when the sangat had his darshan they too were immensely happy. It was a bonus for them.

From a report by Mr Babani

With Mr DeVries and Mrs Wood in the lobby of the West Centre Hotel.

At the information table, and *(below)* child care.

*O*n the path of God-realization, one must become unfettered like a child.

With Mrs Wood, Mr Babani and Mrs Ahuja.

English meeting at the West Centre Hotel in London, with Mr Babani and Mrs F. E. Wood. 1979

Maharaj Ji had a way of turning every question to the sangat's advantage, however foolish or strange the question might seem. Once, someone asked:

Q. Master, is there any bad karma in asking a bad question?
A. Well, if it's a bad karma, it must be my bad karma!

Q. Maharaj Ji, in your estimation, what is a good question to ask?
A. I am more concerned with the good answer which I should give, rather than the good question! A question will never be good, but the answer will always be good! Questions mean that there are doubts to be cleared. So when there are doubts in the mind, how can it be good? But the answer is always, "Attend to your meditation"— and that is always good. Ultimately it is this that will take us back to the Father.

*M*editation is the real prayer. There are no set words with which to pray to the Father; there is no language for communicating with the Father. The heart has no language at all. The heart's language is love.

Saints teach us the real art of praying to the Father. They put us on the path. They tell us how to withdraw our consciousness to the eye centre and how to attach it to the Spirit; how, with the help of the Spirit, we have to make progress through those regions—spiritual progress within—and then come back to the level of the Father. That is real prayer.

Arriving in Los Angeles. 1964

From Maharaj Ji's address to the sangat on May 9, 1964, on his arrival for the first time in the United States of America —

*F*or me, personally, this event is one of considerable significance, not only for the honour being shown to me on a great continent to which I have been able to come for the first time, but more especially because I find myself today on that part of American soil which can claim to have the oldest association with the Dera. It was to the West Coast that Sant Mat first came in the first quarter of this century when someone, on behalf of Hazur Maharaj Ji, our Great Master, initiated the first American. It is here that the Radha Soami philosophy in America slowly took root and where, I think, we have the highest concentration of American satsangis. Sant Mat has a great and promising future in this wonderful country of yours.

Disneyland.

California.

With a group of New York satsangis. 1964

California. 1964

Wherever Maharaj Ji went, people noticed him and asked who he was. Yet he never sought attention. The fact was that his dignity and noble bearing combined with gentleness and good humour in such an extraordinary way that people were drawn to him as to one who possessed a unique and precious treasure. On many occasions—in restaurants, in hotels or even on the street—people asked whether he was a 'maharaja'.

English meeting in Detroit. Seated with Maharaj Ji is his representative, James B. Replogle; standing is Henry Khielhorn. 1964

Satsang in Detroit.

This is not a new philosophy, nor is it confined to any one country or people. It is, in fact, the true heritage of all and is the essence of all religions, which has been lost sight of and forgotten—due, perhaps, to our paying disproportionate attention to material progress. This is now being realized in this country, and I am happy to find that the common motivation of all is the search for peace and harmony, nationally and internationally.

With A.V.M. Sondhi (left), Mr Harry Mutter, and Mrs Madelaine Mutter (right) in Detroit.

Detroit.

Satsangis from all over America gathered in Detroit, Michigan, to take a bus tour with Maharaj Ji to the Ford Motor Company factory at River Rouge, Michigan. The tour was followed by a picnic.

The best way to get rid of worries is to let them die of neglect.

Satsang at Eden's Motel, Chicago. Mr Replogle is seated next to Maharaj Ji. 1964.

Satsang in Chicago. 1964

Dining with satsangis. 1964

Whenever I had asked the Indian satsangi students how they liked American food, they would remark it was very monotonous and dull, as we mostly use only salt and butter to flavour our food. But Maharaj Ji, when asked how he liked American food, lovingly and graciously answered: "It likes me."

Letter from a Detroit satsangi, 1964

Entering satsang in New York. 1964

With A.V.M. Sondhi at satsang in New York. 1964

From Maharaj Ji's address to the New York sangat on June 18, 1964 —

On this occasion I have no particular message to give you except the classical one that Christ left behind for all humanity, which is "Love one another." For the greater the love we have for one another, the closer we are together, to me and to the Lord. It is my hope that the group meetings held at the various centres and the questions and answers following such meetings have brought about a deeper understanding of Sant Mat philosophy. It is my wish that you will devote yourself to your meditation with this renewed knowledge, love and perseverance.

At the Lincoln Memorial, Washington, D.C. 1964

Arrival in Washington, D.C., with Mr and Mrs Weekley. 1970

From a letter to a friend, written in Washington, D.C. on May 21, 1970 —

$\mathcal{B}$y Maharaj Ji's grace my tour is just wonderful from a satsang point of view. People are hungry for spirituality and they realize now that material achievements have not led them to any happiness or peace of mind, and, strange enough, they are not very rigid in their Christian beliefs. They have started thinking openly and are trying to come out from the traditional beliefs. So it is very easy to reach them through the Bible.

I have been reading so much while in India of planes being hijacked to Cuba. Though I have been hovering over these islands around Cuba, I have not been lucky to get this free flight!

Detroit. 1970

Detroit. 1970

In New York, two members of the hotel staff, a plumber and a maid, appeared before Mr Weekley with a bag of tools and a work order to repair a leaking faucet in the bathroom of Maharaj Ji's hotel suite. Mr Weekley told them to wait and, going through the room where Maharaj Ji was giving interviews, checked the bathroom, to find nothing wrong with the taps. "There must be a mistake, the taps are fine," he told them. After a moment's silence the plumber said, "Yes, you are right. We made this up ourselves because we want to see the man with the beautiful eyes."

Mr Weekley was so touched by his guileless confession that, ignoring the line of satsangis waiting outside, he took the plumber and maid into Maharaj Ji's room and said, "Please pardon me, Maharaj Ji, but I could not help bringing these people to see you." The Master got up from his chair before Mr Weekley had finished speaking and stood looking at the couple, a gentle smile on his face. They, for their part, gazed at "the man with the beautiful eyes", neither speaking nor moving. Then the Master shook hands with them and patted them on the shoulder as he said good-bye. They emerged from the Master's room with joy on their faces and tears in their eyes—and they did not even know who he was!

On the morning Maharaj Ji left New York for Detroit, there was a wonderful scene in his hotel corridor: a large number of the hotel workers—maids, waiters, and repairmen, none of them satsangis—had gathered outside the Master's room to say good-bye and have a final glimpse of "the man with the beautiful eyes".

Satsang in New York. 1970

*T*here's only one religion—religion of love for the Lord. Give it any name.

Satsang in Minneapolis, with Janak Puri and Colonel Berg. 1970

On the plane between satsang venues in the U.S.A. 1970

*L*ove doesn't need language to convince anybody. It affects the heart straight and it rebounds from the heart straight. No language is required to express it, nor is reason required to convince yourself that you are in love. You know when you are in love. Why you are in love—you have no explanation for it.

All photos: Pasadena, California. 1970

221

Satsang in Pasadena, with Janak Puri and Roland DeVries. 1970

Letter to the Dera Secretary—Los Angeles, June 28, 1970

My satsang tour in America, by Maharaj Ji's grace, has come to an end, and I think Maharaj Ji's teachings have been well received in every centre I have visited. People seem to be very happy, rather overjoyed, and it pleases me most to see so much love and harmony among the satsangis this time. This has attracted a lot of new seekers and many satsang centres are growing quite rapidly.

It gladdens my heart to find so many youngsters being attracted to the path. There seems to be sort of a revolt against too much hypocrisy from this modern civilization and they want to break from the traditional conventions of the society. There seems to be a great awakening in their hearts, but they try to achieve it with the help of drugs. Let me hope some day their search will lead them to the right direction.

All the representatives and people concerned have made beautiful arrangements for my stay and for the satsangs. I have no words to express my thanks and appreciation for what they have done.

The last two weeks of my tour have been increasingly tiring and exhausting, and today I am looking forward to boarding the ship for Honolulu. It will be a rare occasion for me that for five days I don't have to hold any satsang nor give any interviews or initiations, nor to go on long drives to satsangis' houses or for sightseeing. From now onward my satsang tour will not be too demanding on me and I am looking forward anxiously to being back at the Dera amongst all of you. I don't think I have ever worked so hard on any other satsang tour, but by Maharaj Ji's grace I am keeping fairly good health.

When I left India I had planned not to initiate anybody on this tour, but right from my first stop at Athens I have started initiating practically at every centre. People are so sincere and devoted that I had no heart to refuse them.

... At Detroit I discussed with all the elders about one organization for the whole American continent. They all agreed quite lovingly and willingly, and now I have constituted an assembly of twenty talents of satsangis here in the States to formulate the constitution for that one organization. They will be sending the draft to us at the Dera and, if approved by you and Lala Tara Chand Ji, then they can go ahead with its registration and functioning here.

... If all goes well, I'll be in Bombay on the 14th night and will be in Dera by 17th. I'll wire you my exact date and time of arrival at Dera when I reach Bombay.

With loving regards to you all.

222

En route with Janak Puri.

Dera without the Master—by Daryai Lal Kapur

I have been constantly receiving letters from abroad requesting me to send some Dera news for insertion in their satsang monthlies. But what Dera news could be sent during the last three months, when there was no life in the Dera?

The 'Dera' had gone out of the Dera. They did not want to know what construction works were now in progress at the Dera, or how many houses had recently been added to the new model colony, or when the new tube well would reach completion, or if the design for the new guest house for foreigners had finally been approved, and whether it would consist of forty flats or more.

Neither were they interested to know how the Dera was functioning without the One who was its Life and Light. About a thousand souls still lived there—but were they really living?

My friends, now that you have had some experience of the Master living among you for some time and then leaving you, perhaps you will be able to realize that they were not living.

Those of you who witnessed the Lord travelling incognito in your midst—moving on earth in the human form—will be able to understand to some extent what pangs of separation the residents of Dera suffered during His long absence.

You remark: "Why? He was absent for only two months."

Well, for them it was more than two centuries. One shot by an arrow only knows what the pain of the world is.

Morning and evening they counted the days and hours of his return. Always the same question was put to me: "What is the date today?"

"July 9th," I answered, telling the date for the fiftieth time.

"Ha! Still seven days more."

The questioner will sigh and turn away from me lest I may notice the tears in his or her eyes.

223

Photographing the pyramids. 1970

Surrounded by children. 1970

Next morning, walking down some high, steep, stone staircase of one of the buildings at the pyramids, Master was sighted by a group of about fifty Mexican children, early teenagers and younger, and all brightly dressed. The very same instant they all let out an uninhibited whoop of joy and raced across the eighty yards or so to completely engulf Master at the foot of the stairs. He joined them in their joy, laughing as much as they, caught up in the innocence, catching them up in his soaring, carefree laughter.

Letter from Lionel Metz, May 1970

Satsang. 1970

Arrival at Sydney, Australia, with Bea Jauncey. 1968

On one of Maharaj Ji's tours, a small incident occurred involving Mrs Bea Jauncey. Maharaj Ji was walking on a footpath followed by Professor Puri, Mrs Jauncey and another lady. A man coming from the opposite direction saw him from a distance and started gazing at him. When he came near, with eyes still fixed on the Master's face, he kept on walking and bumped into Mrs Jauncey, almost knocking her down. Without turning to look at her, but pointing to Maharaj Ji, he said, "Sorry! He is responsible for this."

With Bea Jauncey and members of her family in New Zealand. 1968

Satsang in Auckland. Tony and Marilyn Waddicor seated third and fourth from left.

With young Karen Waddicor in New Zealand. 1968

With Bea at Mount Cook airfield, New Zealand. 1968

This I think has been the best day of our trip since leaving India, a day that Maharaj Ji enjoyed most thoroughly. We flew from Christchurch to Milford all through the Southern Alps. The plane, a Dakota, flew us first to Mount Cook airfield where after a brief halt, just 180 seconds, we flew on to Queenstown. Here we changed planes and got into a small seven-seater two-engined biplane. The Dakota was piloted by Bea's nephew. He had taken the plane close to the snowy Alps, but the second pilot of the smaller plane who took us to Milford was a daredevil man. He flew the plane in so close to the mountains that Maharaj Ji had to ask me as to what he was up to, and I thought that he was so close that it was possible to put one's hand out of the window and get a fist full of snow off the slopes. It was a very exciting and thrilling flight. From Milford we flew back to Queenstown and caught the same Dakota back to Christchurch. The Dakota en route did a similar feat to what the smaller plane had done earlier in the day. The pilot took a complete turn around in a small valley to let passengers on both sides have a jolly good look at a beautiful glacier below the plane. To top it all we had a marvellous sunset over the peaks. It had been a cloudless day, one in hundreds, as at this time of the year it is rare for South New Zealand to have a clear day. A perfect day and Maharaj Ji enjoyed every bit of it.

Letter from Madan Mehta, June 22, 1968

Suva, 1968. Maharaj Ji, untypically, gave the hour-long satsang standing.

Noumea. 1968

On 4 July we left the hotel at 8:00 a.m. and travelled along King's Road to Nandi. It was a lovely sight to see all the quaint little villages, neat and tidy, situated under the palms with beautiful lush green grass growing all around. The sugar cane plantations, Fiji's main product, are managed by Indians mostly from the Punjab. We stayed the night in Lautuka and drove to Nandi the next morning to catch a flight to Noumea.

On 8 July, after several days of much-needed rest, we sat waiting in a taxi to take us to the airport for our flight to Singapore. Maharaj Ji mentioned how good everybody had been, and with a smile on his face he said, "What could I have done in my last birth to deserve all the love and affection received everywhere?"

Letter from Madan Mehta, July 16, 1968

With Sam Busa, the representative for South Africa. 1966

With Janak Puri.

Sant Mat came to South Africa at the end of World War II when Sir Colin Garbett, Major Little and Dr Lander retired there after their service with the British government in India. Till 1951, there were only four satsangis in the country. After Maharaj Ji bestowed Nam on a few seekers from South Africa in 1954, the sangat began to grow, and by the end of 1965 there were more than 350 satsangis.

With Sir Colin Garbett.

During one of the informal tea parties, a little girl climbed up into Maharaj Ji's lap. Maharaj Ji looked across at her mother who was sitting nearby. Who knows what happened, but the mother, who was not initiated, fell to the ground. As she got back on her feet she said to her husband who was sitting beside her that she wanted them to go over to Maharaj Ji and ask him for Nam. Just that morning she had eaten fish for breakfast. Husband and wife walked over to Maharaj Ji and the lady requested him to initiate her. "Are you sure you can do without fish and meat?" he asked. She replied that it would be no problem. The next morning, he initiated her.

A satsangi asked the Master, "Could I please know how I am to address Maharaj Ji in private conversation?" The Master leaned towards the questioner with an expression of gentleness and love. "Brother," he said, "we are all travellers on the same path. There is no special form of address. It must be heart to heart."

Johannesburg. 1982

Addressing the South African sangat in 1982 —

I'm quite conscious that I have come here after sixteen years. Not that I didn't want to, but I just couldn't. There were so many factors in my way which were difficult for me to overcome. The moment I got the chance—at the first opportunity—I am here with you all. But in spite of being away, you have all been very near and dear to me.

234

Replying to a question about recognizing a true Master —

$\mathcal{W}$ell, very frankly, it is impossible. It is only by His grace that we can be on the path, and we can be led in the right direction by the right person. It is only by His grace. Our intellect fails here. There are many things which we can discuss intellectually, but they are just said intellectually and heard intellectually. But actually, conviction comes from within. Logic doesn't satisfy us at all. Automatically all our questions are dissolved—all questions vanish—when we are in the presence of the Master. The pull comes from within. We just feel from within that this is the path for us. By our intellect, we can never know.

At a tea party in Chatsworth, with *(above)* the Naidoo family and Mr Bob Attwell. 1982

CHAPTER FOUR

Dera Activities

era Baba Jaimal Singh is situated in Punjab, India, some six kilometres from the national highway that goes northwards from Delhi, through Punjab and on towards Pakistan. When Baba Jaimal Singh first settled there in 1891, it was a lonely, uninhabited wilderness of scrub land and ravines.

By the time Hazur Maharaj Ji passed from this world in 1990, the Dera had become a substantial township. "Baba Ji Maharaj chose this secluded quiet place," he once explained, "so that the spiritual atmosphere of satsang would always be maintained, and the sangat's attention would not be distracted by other pursuits." His words encapsulate the guiding principle that has shaped the growth of the Dera and generated its unique character and atmosphere.

Satsang or the spiritual discourse—the encounter between disciple and Master so necessary for spiritual awakening and inner growth—is the way the saints spread their message of truth. And if we look to history, to the lives of all great spiritual teachers, we see that there are two ways they do this. They travel, sometimes ceaselessly, finding their flock in the context of their own homes. Or they establish a base, where they then attract their followers to come to them.

The Dera over the years has served as the hub for the great wheel of spiritual teaching set in motion by the Beas Masters. All activities there arise, essentially, out of the principle of satsang. In Baba Ji's days, two satsang halls were built and a well sunk to provide pure drinking water. A few small rooms were then built to give shelter to disciples who had come from considerable distances and could not return to their homes on the same day. A langar or free kitchen was established, as is the tradition in India, so that visitors should not face inconvenience with regard to their food. And over the years, as the sangat kept growing, these basic amenities—provision for satsang, shelter for the sangat and food for all—were continuously expanded to ensure that the atmosphere would remain conducive to this basic need for the meeting of Master and disciple.

In anticipation of the rapid growth that was to take place during his mastership, Maharaj Ji from the beginning started a process of continuous and large-scale building work. Incorporating the love of the sangat through mitti and brick seva into the very foundations, he enlarged the langar, built hostels for visitors, residential blocks for the increasing number of permanent sevadars, public toilet facilities and an infrastructure of roads, drainage, power and communications that became the template for all future growth. With the proximity of the river and the sinking of several deep tube wells, water had become plentiful and the barren, dry and dusty terrain was gradually transformed into a shady, comfortable environment.

As he toured the country and attracted more and more disciples, the number of people visiting the Dera for the monthly satsangs continued to swell. Maharaj Ji's love, and his lucid, simple discourses, drew thousands, then hundreds of thousands of visitors to the Dera. To meet the needs of the enormous crowds that were the norm by the eighties, he once again enlarged and reorganized the langar, and constructed large multi-purpose sheds to provide shelter both for satsang and from the elements at night. Proper and ample sanitation facilities were constructed on a large scale, and facilities were provided for the sangat to deposit their personal belongings so they could freely attend satsang and the langar. Eventually, even the grounds of the satsang ghar and the open field behind it proved inadequate for the morning satsang, and a vast open-sided shed was built which could accommodate satsang in any weather.

Maharaj Ji took personal interest in every aspect of the development of the colony, notwithstanding his formidable daily routine of morning satsang, darshan for the sevadars, interviews for groups and individuals, office work and correspondence, and an evening satsang in English for foreign visitors followed by a question-and-answer session. He also gave regular time and attention to the Dera publications, making them a key element in the Society's activities. With the growth in the sangat, he saw that books would play a valuable role in supporting a disciple's spiritual practice, particularly for those who lived far away from the Master or were unable to attend satsang regularly.

While satsang has always been the purpose of the development at the Dera, the material out of which everything has been fabricated must be understood to be nothing but love. Only then does the Dera make sense. Led by a true Master on the path of the saints, each disciple, each sevadar—including the Master, who is the sevadar par excellence—is ultimately engaged in a spiritual love affair, an affair with love itself. The Master demonstrates what this means, as he serves his predecessor—and through his obedience to his Master, he serves the Lord. They are precious links, the Masters—a golden chain of perfect lovers leading to the infinite love that is God. How else could Maharaj Ji serve the sangat in this superhuman way for forty years? And how could men and women from all walks of life discover within themselves stamina they had never dreamt of, as they toiled and laboured day and night to serve each other, to serve their Master, to serve God?

Out of his abundant compassion, Maharaj Ji also undertook several projects to help alleviate the physical suffering of the people. He started by involving the sangat in a blood donation programme in response to the acute shortage of blood faced by the local hospitals. Shortly after this, and moved by the large numbers of people with degrees of blindness that can be treated and improved, he channelled the love of the sangat into the annual Dera Eye Camp which is open to all. When he saw that a permanent medical facility would be of great benefit to the local population and to those patients who could not be treated within the limitations of an eye camp, he again engaged the sangat to build the 300-bed Maharaj Sawan Singh Charitable Hospital just six kilometres from the Dera. During the mid-1980s, when terrorism created hardships and insecurity throughout the Punjab, Maharaj Ji opened the gates of Dera to all refugees who wanted help, providing them with shelter, food, and schooling for their children as long as they stayed. After the completion of the Beas hospital in 1986, he started a second hospital in Sikanderpur, Haryana.

His love was limitless. Though it spilled over far and wide, the sangat were the chief beneficiaries for they could always reap its bounty through the opportunities he gave them to serve.

The purpose of satsang, of holding meetings, is to strengthen our faith and meditation—to create an atmosphere in which to build our meditation. If there are any doubts, questions or obstacles, they just get answered, dissolved, resolved; we are then able to hold that atmosphere in which we have to build our meditation. That is the main purpose of satsang. It is no ritual or ceremony. Just by attending a satsang you will not get anything—that's wrong. You carry home the atmosphere of the satsang and attend to your meditation; that will give you everything. The doubts of your mind that you have been able to resolve and dissolve in the satsang—that is going to give you everything. The faith which the satsang builds in you and the devotion it builds in you, that gives you everything.

Early 1960s

Recalling the Great Master, who had built the satsang ghar —

*T*his whole Dera reflects his story. From everybody's lips and eyes you will find his life. This whole place radiates love and devotion that is all his.

Arriving at morning satsang in the 1970s.

Morning satsang. 1969

1974

Satsang in the satsang ghar.

*O*nly that is satsang where the teachings of the one Shabd and Nam are proclaimed, where the desire to find and love the Lord is awakened, and where the way or method of true worship is explained.

*T*here's only one way to subdue the mind, to rub it with the Shabd every day. Just as when there is rust on a knife, you rub it on a sandstone and slowly and slowly the rust goes and the knife shines.

Satsang in the multi-purpose shed. Late 1980s

Bhandara satsang. December 29, 1976

Explaining the significance of the word *bhandara* in the Dera context —

*B*handara means free langar, where free food is served to everybody. Here every day is a bhandara—nobody is charged for meals. In Dera we run a free langar every day. But we have certain days when we gather in memory of the Great Master, in memory of Baba Jaimal Singh Ji, and we call them bhandaras. One is December 29 when Baba Ji parted from this earth. We always have a gathering on that particular day, irrespective of whether it is Sunday or Monday. Since Great Master's time we have been gathering on that day. Call them conventions or traditions—they have been created by the Great Master, not by me.

Call them bhandaras, call them monthly satsangs, it is same thing. They started from the Great Master's time because he used to be in service for probably eleven years after becoming the Master. Being still in service, he selected certain days and told satsangis and devotees, "I'll be here in Dera on these days for satsang so people may come to hear satsang." The rest of the time he was doing his job. The particular days when he would be in Dera— that was always the last Sunday of the month. In between, he might come if he got leave, but on those particular days, he saw to it that he would be there. The sangat knew he would be there so they would gather from all the villages and cities to hear his discourses. So that is how the tradition started, and it continued after he retired from government service, and it is being continued even today. People know that on these days I'll definitely be here.

Speaking of the continuous growth of the sangat —

𝒴ou see, the seed of a banyan tree is very small. But, when the banyan tree grows, so many birds, so many animals, so many people, sit under the shade of that tree. But to begin with, the seed is very small. This foundation started with that hut that Baba Ji built here. Now you can see the hut—how it has expanded.

O brave friend, catch hold of the Master's cloak,
for he is above all ups and downs.
He will be with you both here and hereafter,
in this world of mind and matter, and beyond.
Rumi

English meeting with overseas visitors in Maharaj Ji's drawing room.

English meeting with Professor Bhatnager. Late '60s

Referring in a letter to his heavy schedule and the increasing number of foreign guests in the seventies —

*O*ur guest house is full of foreigners from practically all nationalities, and they keep me quite occupied with their personal problems, interviews and evening meetings. My duties start early in the morning at about 3:30-4:00 o'clock and end at 10:00 at night. Except for one hour's break after lunch, I am always on my toes, running about, attending to people. Unfortunately, there is no 'Sunday' for me, and the question of a holiday does not arise.

Wearing Great Master's coat.

Referring to the question of meeting the living Master, Maharaj Ji wrote
to one of his disciples —

*O*nce you have been initiated into the technique, the practice can
be carried on anywhere, irrespective of geographical differences.
Of course, it is an advantage to be in the presence of the Master.

259

English meetings in the upstairs room in the International Guest House. 1970s

In these intimate gatherings with the foreigners, Maharaj Ji revealed his human face—his compassion, his humility and, to the delight of the sangat, his down-to-earth and wonderful sense of humour. A disciple once said: "When I look at you at satsang, I see you sometimes very shiny and bright. Is this only my imagination, or is it His grace?" Maharaj Ji with a straight face replied, "There may be some light at my back, some electric bulb or something?"

Not only was he humorous to the point that he sometimes made the sangat cry with laughter—he was also the epitome of patience. People would pose all manner of questions, some foolish, some embarrassing, some even insulting. Maharaj Ji met them all with the same even-handedness and love. Once asked to define patience, he replied: "Howsoever unreasonable the questions may be, howsoever odd they may be, you go on attending to them smilingly. That is patience."

Once a lady got up in the meeting and said she would like to marry him. He replied that he was already married. In that case, she said, she would like to have an affair with him. "Sister," he replied, "we are already having an affair. A spiritual affair." On yet another occasion, a lady got up and said over and over again to him, "I love you, I love you, I love you." Maharaj Ji did not interrupt her. When eventually she had emptied her heart, he responded simply, "Sister, you didn't say 'only'."

261

In Maharaj Ji's garden.

Outside the satsang ghar.

In his garden. 1970s

1968

Morning darshan on the Guest House lawn. 1978

In the English meetings, Maharaj Ji often teased the Westerners in response to their uninhibited questions:

Q. Master, what is it about us that makes you sad?

A. Your miserable faces. Your woeful tales and horrible letters. Naturally, such letters can never brighten you, they just depress you.

Q. What makes you happy?

A. You people make me happy—you people make me sad.

Q. How do we make you happy?

A. With your smiling faces.

Daily satsangs in English were held in the evening for the benefit
of overseas visitors and took the form of a talk given by Maharaj Ji
or Prof. Bhatnagar, followed by a period of informal questions and
answers. In the fifties, when the number of foreign visitors was
very small, these meetings would be held in Maharaj Ji's own sitting
room. As the number increased, the satsang was moved to the upstairs lounge of the International Guest House. By the eighties,
this too proved inadequate, and a domed tent was created in the
guest house garden with a seating capacity of some several hundred.

"Be not proud of your intelligence!" cautioned the wise one. "Did you not hear
of the ant on a leaf in a mud puddle who thought he was captain of a ship on
an ocean? Did you not meet the condemned man who knew everything about
his prison cell?"

English meeting in the Guest House compound. 1984

A group of satsangis from the mountainous Kulu region were given a group darshan during their visit to Dera. As it was raining outside, the Guest House dining room was cleared and rugs were put down for them. When Hazur came into the room, everyone spontanously started crying—it was one of those charged atmospheres which made your hair stand on end, so intense was their love and devotion. Some of them were permitted to approach Maharaj Ji to speak to him, but they could not say anything; they just cried and cried and cried.

From an account by Madan Mehta, 1982

269

Initiation selection.

For it is not what you are or have been
that God looks at with his merciful eyes,
but what you would be.
                    The Cloud of Unknowing

Just as fire is latent in wood
And can be produced with skill;
So is the flame of God's Name
Latent in everyone,
And can be revealed
Through the Guru's wisdom.

Kasat men jyo hai baisantar
math sanjam kadh kadhijai,
Ram nam hai jot sabai
tat gurmat kad laieje.
                    Adi Granth

Initiation selection. 1986

272

Walking through the langar. 1975

Speaking of the spiritual purpose underlying the langar and other amenities —

*O*ne of the objects of running the langar is to provide an opportunity to the satsangis to serve others. It increases mutual love and understanding amongst the satsangis. It enables them to rise above the narrow distinctions of the rich and the poor, of the high and the low.

I do not know how and from where all this food came. Right from my childhood I have always seen the langar storehouse full of grain. Now, there is ample grain in our stocks and a great deal more than our needs, inspite of the fact that lakhs and lakhs of people are fed in the free langar every day, especially during our monthly satsangs. It is all thanks to the love and devotion of the sangat that the Dera management does not have to buy any food grains from the market.

Leaving his house to visit the langar.

Every bhandara, as the crowds came into the Dera and ate in the langar, Maharaj Ji made twice-daily tours of the entire area. He would walk from his house and then go from section to section, ending in the hall where vast numbers of chapatis were stacked. As he moved from one part of the langar to the next, he would stop for a few minutes in front of the groups of sevadars to give them darshan. The atmosphere would be so charged, only a heart of stone could fail to be moved.

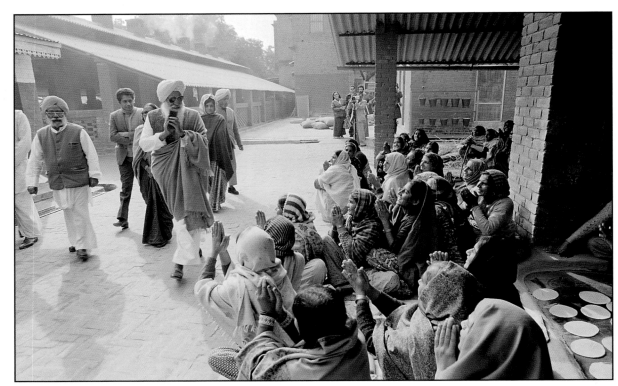
Sevadars making the chapatis. 1978

*Y*ou must have witnessed so many ladies cooking, how they cook just by the side of the fire. In winter it is all right, but imagine the month of June and July when it is so humid and hot. You can't see the fire, you can't sit near it and yet they cook even more than what you have witnessed here. And yet they are so happy, so contented. The spirit to serve the sangat is always there with them. It is all Baba Ji's grace you see....

$\mathcal{W}$ho's the host and who's the guest? I don't know! Satsangis are the host, satsangis are the guest. They come, they cook, they eat and they go—I don't know whom to thank. Whether I have to thank them, or they have to thank me, I've never been able to know.

Now more than 200,000 people collect in the colony. [The present numbers are nearer to 500,000.] You know it's not a very ordinary job, it's a tremendous job for their stay, for their food, for their bath, so many other things one needs. Everybody's looked after. Who looks after them, how they look after them, I don't know at all. I don't know whether I have to thank the sangat, or they have to thank me, I don't know. I've never been able to know. And I even don't know who does it. They think I do it, I think they do it. I'm grateful to them; they come and thank me. I don't know why.

Blessing chapatis in the langar. 1989

Leaving the langar with S. S. Bhandari (holding the umbrella).

1989

With Brigadier Bal. 1989

*P*arshad has no spiritual significance except it reminds you of the Master, of the teachings and of your meditation, and it creates that love and devotion for the Father, for the Master. It should induce you to attend to your meditation and remain steadfast on the principles of Sant Mat. We often keep pictures of our friends at home; we have certain gifts given to us by our friends. What is the advantage of those gifts? They are just to remind us of our friends, of their friendship, of their love for us, nothing else. So similarly parshad also reminds us of the Master, of his love, of our love and devotion for the Master. It should induce us towards meditation; that is the advantage of parshad.

283

*Y*ou see your own reflection in the Master. If you have love
and devotion, you will feel he's in love with you—he loves
you. If you are indifferent to him, you'll feel your Master is
indifferent to you. This is our own reflection.

Blessing puffed rice to be distributed among the sangat.

Each year Maharaj Ji gave parshad to the permanent sevadars.

Maharaj Ji's driver, Malkiat Singh, receiving parshad from him.

Colonel Hardyal (in white waistcoat) and S. S. Bhandari (to Maharaj Ji's left).

Maharaj Ji serving food—his mother is standing in the background.

Serving Cuckoo, with Mr Naidu and Shoti in line.

Soon after he became Master, Maharaj Ji instituted the yearly occasion of 'sadhu's lunch', which continues right up to today. All the permanent sevadars residing in the Dera are invited to eat at the Master's home as guests of his family, and he and the family members serve them.

Maharaj Ji serving the second row from the left. Those who are not seated are family members helping to serve.

At the dining table of mercy
Thou has been treating me like an honoured guest
And urging me to take many helpings of thy mercy.
I tried to outdistance thy grace by my transgressions,
But I stand defeated; thy generosity perplexes me.

Sarmad

Maharaj Ji and members of his family about to eat after serving everyone at the sadhus' lunch.

A tea party for the Dera school children in Maharaj Ji's garden. To Maharaj Ji's left is Mrs Kamal Bagai. In the background (*L-R*) are S. L. Sondhi, Prof. Narang, Madan Gopal Singh, and Harjeet.

The master planner!

With devotion as your shield, rule your body;
Use wisdom as the weapon to fight your war—
This is the way of the man of true valour.
With forgiveness as his scimitar, he sways the world;
He conquers humanity with the sword of love.
He routs the forces of attachment, pride and greed,
He is victorious over the foes of lust and anger.
He is the king of kings, says Paltu,
He rules with glory the three worlds.
Such, indeed, is the man of true valour.

Paltu

Morning mist rises over the Dera.

There was nothing built in the Dera that Maharaj Ji did not personally inspect. Each and every road, each and every building—he walked there and gave it his particular and personal attention.

The construction of "B" and "C" block residential houses.

Inspecting a construction site.

With Mr Bolakani, Maharaj Ji's first sevadar to take the role of chief engineer.

Throughout Maharaj Ji's years as Master, the Dera expanded its boundary walls continuously to accommodate the ever-expanding needs of the sangat. Housing, hostels, sheds, and amenities, everything had to increase. In his last year, responding to a question about the tremendous spurt in growth of the colony during the previous five years, Maharaj Ji said: "We are still enlarging and have not reached the final boundary yet. I know the farm is about 1,000 acres, most of it planted with trees, and about 350 to 400 acres with vegetables. Trees are the breathing lungs of man. They look wonderful and are beautiful, and give protection to the birds."

Inspecting the construction of a multi-purpose shed.

Inspecting the construction of an outer boundary wall.

To meet the needs of the sangat, Maharaj Ji undertook the construction of multi-purpose sheds. These vast covered areas, designed and fabricated at the Dera, are basically an open steel skeleton with a lightweight roof and open sides. The sides are then partially built in, with bricks and cement lattice-screens, to enclose the structure. The average shed can sleep about 25,000—each with its own bath and toilet facilities. A special shed was also built to hold satsang when the weather is not suitable for an outdoor satsang, with a seating capacity of some 90,000 people.

Early days, walking round the Dera with S. S. Bhandari (left) and Dev Prakash (right).

Returning from afternoon seva with Dr Stone. 1970s

The Master and disciple: there are compulsions on both sides. Both behave according to their nature, as in the story of the saint who saved a drowning scorpion. When the scorpion stung him, the Master's companion asked him why he had taken the trouble to rescue the scorpion, since it would definitely sting. The Master replied that just as the scorpion had to be true to its nature, he too had to be true to his nature. So Maharaj Ji would step out from his house, to attend to the welfare of the sangat, and the sangat would surround him and make it impossible for him to do his work in the way he wanted.

Maharaj Ji spoke in the 1980s of how, as the sangat increased, he gradually became a prisoner of the sangat's love, and found himself more and more restricted in fulfilling his daily routine.

I cannot go out. I cannot walk on the roads in the colony, I can't do anything—I can't see people working, serving. What more of a prisoner can one be? As a policeman takes a person to the jail, locks him up, then when he wants him to go out he collects him from the gate and takes him out again, so it happens with me every day. A little five or ten minutes I get free when you are all sitting in satsang in the morning. Then I take a round of the colony everyday. That is the only time I can see work—what improvement we should do—planning what we can do for the betterment of the management. That is the only time. A spider weaves its own net; then it finds itself a prisoner of that net.

*H*e knows best!

Mitti seva

*M*aster is within every disciple—whether they are five, or whether they are five million. Everybody's Master is with him.

301

*S*eva should help us to meditate. Seva is to clean the vessel so that it can be filled with that nectar within. Seva helps us, cleans us, and then makes the utensil ready to be filled. We have to do the meditation to fill it. Seva cannot take the place of meditation.

With Dr Stone. 1966

With Chacha Ji.

Maharaj Ji used to say that just as some
people take tranquillizers to unwind, so
he had the company of Chacha Amar
Singh. For Maharaj Ji, he was the perfect
companion. Not only was Chacha Ji a
jovial and fun-loving man by nature, but
he also had an unfailing ability to gauge
the need of the moment. A distant relative
of Maharaj Ji's, he would entertain him
with his great sense of humour or he
would remain silent if silence was called
for. Maharaj Ji loved his company and took
him frequently on his travels in India.

With Mr Barkat Ram, the chief engineer. 1975

Maharaj Ji would sit at mitti seva for up to two hours in the after-
noons, and during that time, he would attend to many other duties.
He would conduct interviews, dictate letters, attend to administrative matters and work with his sevadars on current projects such as
books, or the planning of the hospital. Sometimes he would use
this time as an opportunity to catch up with his reading, or with his
close friends, and sometimes he would simply watch the sangat
working. The sangat, for their part, carrying baskets of earth on
their heads, would orient their numerous journeys to have maximum
darshan, and this was their pleasure.

Discussing plans during seva for the Beas hospital.

With *(L-R)* Mr Barkat Ram and the architects—John Rhone, P. B. Mistry and John Templer.

Many hours were spent during seva planning the hospital. It was to be very modern in concept and design and the architects kept coming up with facades that were also very modern. None of their modern designs found favour with Maharaj Ji and this, understandably, made the architects quite unhappy. Maharaj Ji then made his reasoning very clear. "The hospital is not for you and not for me. It is for the simple people who will come for treatment. So we don't want the building to look intimidating or strange, no matter how beautiful it may be. Personally, I like your designs. But we want the building to appeal to them."

Inspecting a model of the hospital in the cold of winter.

With Brigadier Bal and K. L. Khanna…

… with Mr Babani …

… attending to correspondence with Prof. Bhatnagar.

Catching up with office work. 1977

Meeting with the publications committee: Mr K. S. Narang, Mr V. K. Sethi, and Professor J. Puri. 1979

I keep fit because I don't do what I shouldn't do!

311

To the disciples who were always asking for words of wisdom, the Sufi Master said, "Wisdom is not expressed in words. It reveals itself in action." But when he saw them plunge headlong into activity he laughed aloud and said, "That isn't action; that is motion."

With Mr B. K. Sethi.

*I*f you give your problem to the Master, then there's no problem. We give it to him to solve it—but we remain obsessed with the problem. That's not giving it to the Master.

With Lalri Shahani.

With Bea Jauncey. 1968

Bea and Maharaj Ji corresponded regularly. In a letter of 1967, Bea had written to him: "My goodness, Maharaj Ji, you are terribly busy these days, and I simply don't know how you do it all. Any other person would have a nervous breakdown; and you keep going, doing more and more all the time. And no one ever hears a complaint from you."

Meeting with Lionel Metz and his family.

On being asked by a foreign disciple to go with him on his return back home, Maharaj Ji replied with characteristic humour:

You want to abduct me to the United States? There's a lot of checking at the immigration department. They won't allow me like that. So you have to conceal me in such a place that nobody knows you are taking me.

North India, with its extreme climate and seasonal rainfall, is basically a dust bowl wherever it is not irrigated or forested. Nowadays, when most of the Dera is paved or cultivated, one can easily forget how dusty it was in earlier times. During the bhandaras in particular, visitors coming to the Dera in the thousands would raise a pall of dust that would hang over the colony through day and night. Possibly aggravated by this, in his later years, Master often suffered from a bad throat or cough. When anyone expressed concern for his health, he would gently brush them aside, saying: "These ailments are the natural decorations of a body my age."

Inspecting a construction site with the Ghuman *jatha* (group of sevadars).

Giving darshan to sevadars next to the multi-purpose shed.

Photographing the sangat bringing grass for langar fuel from far out in the Beas river bed. 1970s

Crossing a small stream on his return from grass seva.

Maharaj Ji never spared himself, and his stamina was legendary. Those who had personal association with him recall many times when he was still ready to go on, whilst others, much younger than himself, were exhausted.

Their bodies are in the world,
But their souls are with the Lord;
Their bodies are tied to earth,
But their souls are beyond the seven skies.

Attending to office work with the help of Professor Bhatnagar and Diwan Sahib.

Reflecting once on how Great Master had prepared him —

*H*ere my legal knowledge helps me. I often wondered why Great Master made my legal practice so short when I had made my name in law. Then he sent me to the farm. Both subjects helped me in the Dera. Law helped me—buying lands, dealing with revenue records. Farming helped me in taking care of the Dera farms.

Working with Diwan Sahib in the initiation breaks.

Attending to correspondence with Professor Bhatnagar.

Meeting with Dev Prakash during the initiation breaks. 1966

In his office. 1960s

When preparing material for books or just penning his thoughts, Maharaj Ji would typically write in longhand on small pieces of note paper. He would then give the notes to Louise Hilger, who typed them for him. They were later compiled into the different books, and also used for drafting replies to various letters.

To have success in
meditation, the aspirant
must enter upon it with
the determination to explore
its possibilities. He must not
start with reservations, but
should be ~~prepared~~ willing to
go where he is led but
without expectations. The
essence of meditation is one
pointedness to merge in the
Shabad to the exclusion
of all other thoughts even
when they happen to be
enticing.

331

With Professor Narang. Seva Singh, Mrs Bharat Ram and Madan Gopal Singh are in the background.

With S. S. Bhandari.

With (L-R) R. N. Mehta, Madan Gopal Singh, Colonel Ranbir Singh, Brigadier Bal and Brigadier Dhillon.

With Mr Barkat Ram.

What was it like to work with him? He was a patient listener, treating all alike—young or old, sevadar or friend. Never did he expose anyone's weakness. Ever gracious, ever loving, if you suggested something he disagreed with, he would bring you around to his point of view without belittling you.

Leaving Great Master's house.

Every aspect of his life was referred to Great Master. All credit was passed on to him, as though Maharaj Ji himself was transparent. Even a common courtesy, "How do you do, Maharaj Ji?" gave him the opportunity to remember him as he replied: "I am not doing—it is all his doing. With his grace, I am going comfortably through this life." With the passing years, living like this with every breath, he became more and more identified with his Master—as though there was no separate identity.

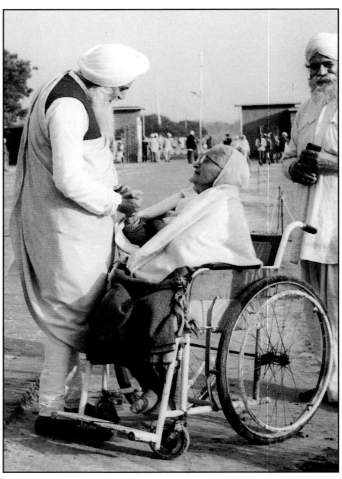

We should become a practical example, a model, before others. That will influence people more than all our persuasion, all our teachings, all our lectures.

With Satguru Jagjit Singh Ji and other visitors from the Namdhari centre.

If you really submit to the Lord, really surrender your
mind to the Lord, if you give yourself to the Lord—
then you don't have to do anything at all. You have no
responsibilities in whatever you may do.

1967

1976

340

How many times and in how many ways did Maharaj Ji caution us against externalizing the saints' spiritual message! Why did he seal the well that had been built by Great Master? Because the sangat had started to ritualize it. This inclination to establish rituals, to interpret physically what the Masters communicate to us spiritually, seems to be part of human nature. The Masters point to a higher level. We busy ourselves with the pointing finger.

Meeting with sevadars in his garden.

Maharaj Ji took the shortcomings of his sevadars upon himself. If there was a problem, he held himself to blame. In his unfailing graciousness, he consistently overpraised the sevadars—inspiring them to do better. The poet speaks of "damning with feint praise". Maharaj Ji did the opposite. He redeemed with praise given in far greater measure than it was deserved.

With sevadars *(L-R):* Professor Bhatnager, K. L. Khanna, Tara Chand Aggarwal, Diwan Sahib and Dev Prakash. Early '70s

With Colonel Berg. 1960

… Sir Colin Garbett. 1967

… Dr Stone.

… Madan Mehta. 1974

L-R: Janak Puri, Louise, Prof. Bhatnagar, V. K. Sethi, Maharaj Ji, A.V.M. Sondhi, Prof. Narang, S. L. Sondhi. 1986

With R. D. Ahluwalia.

International Guest House. 1968

Maharaj Ji loved the 'group photograph'. With friends, family, sevadars and sangat, he would get everyone together, put himself somewhere at the centre and have a picture taken. These disparate groups, the 'children' of his family, were recorded for posterity with their father providing the bond of love.

Dera sevadars.

With Sam Busa, Lesley, and their daughters.

With a group affectionately called 'the hippies'. *L-R:* Bud McKee, Barbara Andino, Mike Nail, William Pryor. 1967

With Dr Naidoo and Dr T. N. Mathur.

With Dr J. M. Pahwa, senior surgeon of the Dera eye camp since its inception.

With Dr and Mrs Bharat Ram.

With Madan Mehta and R. C. Mehta.

With Mr and Mrs Jindal.

With the Governor of Punjab, Shri Mohan Chowdhary (fifth from right).

With the Home Minister of Punjab, Pandit Mohan Lal.

Front row (L-R): Baba Partap Singh Ji, Chief Minister Punjab Darbara Singh, Maharaj Ji, Minister Punjab Ram Kishan, Shoti.

With the Governor of Punjab, S. S. Ray, and Mr Desai after the Dera was reopened to foreigners.
April 1989

Board of Trustees of the Maharaj Jagat Singh Medical Relief Society, 1984. *Standing, L-R:* Brig. Bhalla, Mr D. N. Pathak, Mr S. Balani, Mrs M. Singla, Capt. P. S. Grewal, Mr Seva Singh, Mr K.H. Bhalla, Dr T. N. Mathur.
Seated, L-R: Mr K. S. Narang, Dr Dhillon, Mr T. K. Sethi, Maharaj Ji (Patron), Mr S. R. Jindal, Dr Irani, Mr S. N. Kholi.

Board of Trustees of the Radha Soami Satsang Beas Society, 1989. *Standing, L-R:* Mr R. N. Mehta, Mr K. L. Bhargava, Diwan Iqbal Nath, Mr P. S. Mann, Mr S. L. Sondhi, Brig. K. S. Dhillon, Mr S. R. Katoch, Mr S. R. Jindal, Mr P. K. Desai, Mr Barkat Ram, Mr B. N. Sethi, Justice M. S. Joshi, Mr M. G. Singh, A.V. M. Sondhi, Mr J. P. Bhargava.
Seated, L-R: Mr N. K. Gosain, Mr K. Babani, Mrs S. Bharat Ram, Maharaj Ji (Patron), Mrs I. Rajwade, Prof. K. S. Narang, Brig. G. S. Bal.

*I*t is by His grace that we get an opportunity to do seva. Everybody can't get the opportunity of doing seva. It is entirely His grace that we are capable and we get an opportunity to do seva. Many people may be wanting it, may be anxious to do it, but they never get an opportunity. Their circumstances or family commitments don't permit them; their environment or atmosphere doesn't permit them. It is by His grace that we get this opportunity.

356

Maharaj Ji leaving the blood donation camp.

Testing Maharaj Ji's blood type.

Recalling the Dera blood donation camp —

The first time we held it, probably eight or nine teams came to collect the blood. There were so many donors they couldn't cope with it. And when they sent it to the laboratory, they sent a message: Are you sure it's human blood? They wouldn't believe that so much blood could be given. We had to thoroughly screen people because everybody was anxious to give.

Visiting the Dera Hospital.

The Dera Hospital, now run by the Maharaj Jagat Singh Medical Relief Society, was established in 1958 as a small, 16-bed hospital, inside the Dera, for treating the growing number of residents and to provide medical aid during the bhandaras. The hospital provides free, on-the-spot medical care. At bhandara time it runs a number of first-aid stations around the Dera to take care of the routine medical problems of the visiting crowds, and a small out-patient department. There is also the Nature Cure Hospital, which provides free treatment according to the principles of naturopathy.

Entrance to the Nature Cure Hospital.

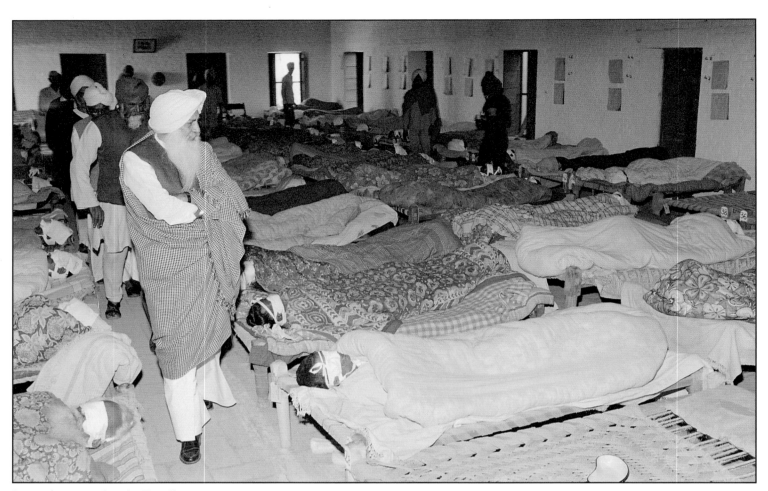

Inspecting a ward at the Eye Camp.

During his many tours through India, Maharaj Ji had become aware of the large number of people suffering from eye disease, especially cataracts, which can be remedied so the person does not become blind. Bibi Ralli had also suggested to Maharaj Ji that the sangat should provide quality medical help to the poor, since there was very little available to them. So in 1965 Maharaj Ji organized the first annual Dera Eye Camp around two basic principles: it would be free of charge (including food and lodging), and it would be open to all.

From the first, the responsibility of Chief Eye Surgeon was placed in the capable and experienced hands of Dr J. M. Pahwa who was then Chief Medical Officer at Gandhi Eye Hospital, Aligarh. In Maharaj Ji's words he was "a good and humble soul, expert in his job, calm, always at peace. So he won people with his devotion to duty and service."

For the first camp, 1,250 patients were operated on. By the 1990s, over 7,000 operations were being successfully completed at each camp by a medical team of some 600 personnel—including doctors, nurses and paramedical technicians. The most notable feature of the camp, remarked on by everyone who has visited it, is the extraordinary spirit of service that permeates everything connected with it.

With Dr Pahwa.

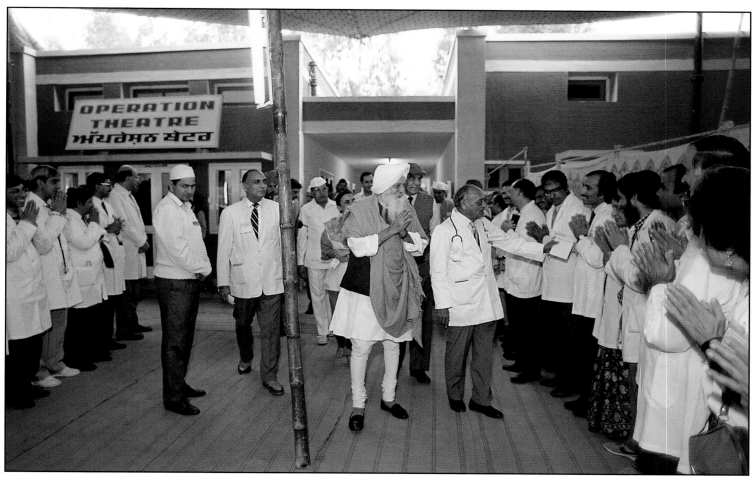

Greeting the doctors and surgeons before the operations commence. 1989

Watching the eye operations being conducted in the operating theatre. 1989

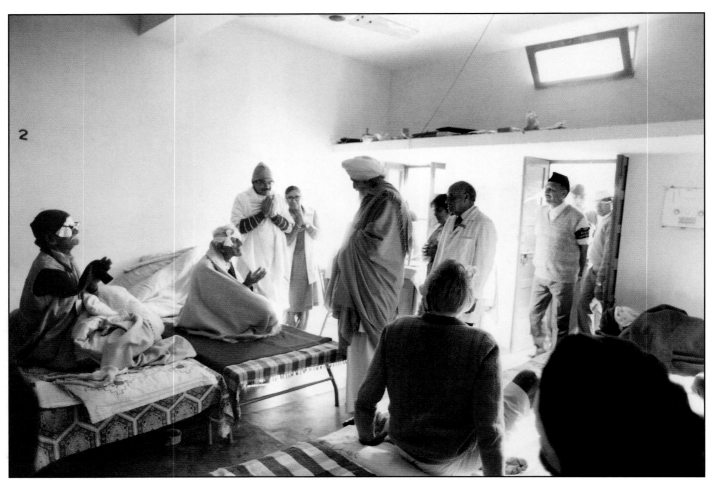

Visiting elderly patients.

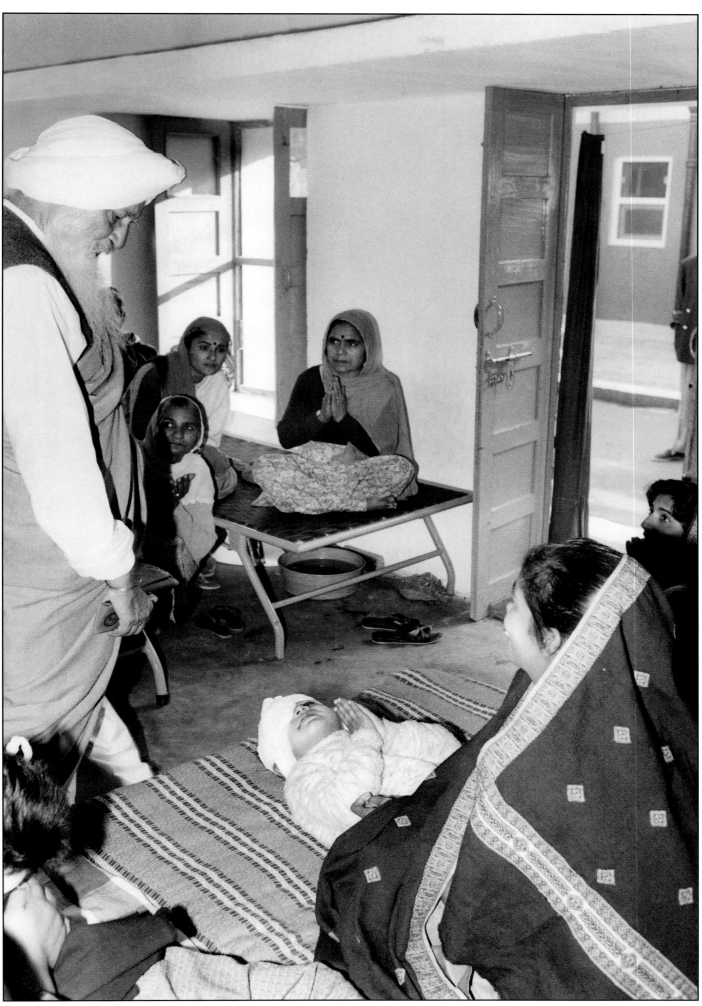

Visiting the children's ward. 1989

Darshan for the patients being discharged.

In his address to mark the completion of one of the eye camps, Maharaj Ji praised the sevadars, saying that there was nothing like it in the world. The atmosphere was electrified—sevadars started sobbing and crying.

The foundation of Dera was laid by Baba Ji Maharaj and Shri Hazur Maharaj Ji on love, seva, humility and meditation. In Dera all are equal—rich and poor, women and men, of any race, of any religion. There is no question of caste or creed. This Dera belongs to all, to every satsangi.

The love with which the sangat serves the eye patients is but a noble example of these principles. The love and devotion with which you have served the eye patients this year and have served them every year—I am not exaggerating—has hardly a parallel in the world. I am not used to making long speeches. I am only used to folding my hands before Hazur Maharaj Ji.

Now, too, I fold my hands before him to beg that he continues to bless his sevadars to serve the eye patients, as in previous years, and likewise to shower his grace on me and his sangat.

Sevadars' parshad. 1989

The atmosphere was so charged when Maharaj Ji praised the sevadars—
they themselves were grateful to him for letting them serve, for letting
them experience a love without bounds—and now he was thanking them.
Himself the supreme example of selfless service, of compassion and right-
mindedness, the living Master serves as a catalyst for others to discover this
ocean of love within themselves. Thus, as Maharaj Ji would remind the
sangat, the real beneficiary of seva is not the patient or the institution but
the one serving.

"It is one's great good fortune," he told the eye camp sevadars, "to get
this opportunity to do seva. It is the Lord's boundless grace, and we should
thank the patients for giving the Dera sangat this chance to serve." Such
was his greatness; such was his humility.

The Beas hospital complex.

In 1978, Maharaj Ji called for a committee to begin planning the construction of a charitable, top-quality hospital that would provide free medical care all year long and would serve all people equally. In his wisdom, he wanted the hospital to be situated some distance from the Dera, so that patients availing of the free care would not feel obligated to visit the Dera, and only those who really wanted to would make the effort. A 35-acre site was therefore selected about seven kilometres from Dera, near the national highway for ease of access.

Work on the building was started in January 1980, and the hospital was inaugurated six years later. The main building is 320,500 square feet and has a capacity of 300 beds. The entire complex consists of residential hostels, residential housing blocks, a community centre, a shopping complex and a bhojan bhandar.

Reviewing the hospital layout ground plan with the engineers.

367

Inspecting the casting of a roof slab.

A Monument of Love

The dedication of the sevadars to seva, their desire to accomplish the maximum in the minimum possible time, is unbelievable. During the time we were still digging the foundations, the sevadars approached the Master and said, "Maharaj Ji, please ask the engineers to put lights on the spot where we are digging." When asked why they needed the lights, they submitted, "Hazur, we are hardly able to do much during the day's work and so much still has to be done. We want to work for a few hours during the night also." And when the Master declined their request with a loving smile, their faces reflected their disappointment.

Curious passersby at the site sometimes wonder at the power that makes the sevadars move with such energy and speed. At times I too feel amazed, only to remember the next moment that the sevadars derive energy from their devotion for the Master—inspired by his omnipresent grace and love. In all these months, never have I seen the sevadars complaining about the hardships of life at the construction site, made all the more difficult by the inclemencies of the weather. During the last sixteen months they have faced rain and storm, hail and frost, and the hot summer winds. They have lived in tents, under freshly laid damp roofs, under awnings, on the rough floors of the unfinished corridors. They have often been drenched by icy showers in winter and have been almost baked by the blazing sun and hot winds in the tropical summer. But nothing can shake them from their rock-like dedication to seva. It is not in their nature to complain. There is only one exception: on some days, when some of us are feeling elated, almost proud, at finishing the day's work early, one of the spokesmen of the sevadars comes and complains, almost in an accusing tone, "Sir, you are not giving us enough work, we are sitting idle."

Viewing the facade of the hospital during its construction. 1984

I feel very small again. Yes, no one can give enough work to them, for they sometimes finish a day's work in a few hours. They will not stop for rest, they take the minimum time off for lunch, and I wonder if they ever feel tired. One day, seeing an old sevadar well over sixty working without a stop, I went up to him and said, "My good friend, please take a few minutes' rest—I've seen you working for the last few hours without a break even to gain your breath. You must be feeling tired." "Tired," he repeated in a hurt voice, "I am not tired. If you could give me seva for the next twelve hours, I would be grateful and happy to do it." And turning away, he was again engrossed in his task.

I pondered; he was right. Does a mother feel tired or complain when she keeps a day-and-night vigil over her sick child? Does a lover grudge to do the bidding of the beloved, however hard it may be? I have heard old satsangis say that if a disciple does seva with a spirit of surrender, if his approach is that of love and devotion, and he has only one desire in his heart—the desire to please his Master—he will not feel tired. And is the Master not serving his disciples with the same spirit of love: never stopping, never complaining, ever vigilant, accepting all the toil and hardships of the arduous task of looking after his flock of sheep with an unflinching concern, with an ever-loving, kind smile?

It has been a privilege for all of us to see his inspiring power, blending with the devotion of his children and taking the shape of beams and columns, walls and lintels, and day after day growing into a monument of love and devotion.

Mr K. H. Bhalla, Project Engineer

369

Discussing the facade. 1985

To test the designs, Maharaj Ji had some full size mock-ups of the arches made on the site, and also of the jalousie, or jali—block panels above the main entrance. One of the architects was trying to explain the aesthetic approach that they were hoping to achieve. "You see, your eyes will be drawn up to the screen by the light shining through it" he said. Then Maharaj Ji, with one of his mischievous smiles remarked, "And if you raise your eyes a little higher, then everything will be full of light."

Giving darshan to a group of hospital construction sevadars.

Meeting with the architects and engineers at the hospital site.

Parshad for hospital construction sevadars seated inside a hospital building still under construction.

Speaking of serving others —

*I*f we can do anything to help anybody, we should. That is our duty. We are meant to help each other. Humans are meant to help humans—who else will help? Birds and lions will not come to help you! You have to help each other. We should be a source of strength to each other, but we should not be involved with the suffering of another person to the extent that we start suffering ourselves—that we ourselves become miserable. We must be strong enough not to be affected. We have to be very helpful, kind and compassionate to them, and help them with their problems.

Touring the hospital complex after its official opening. 1986

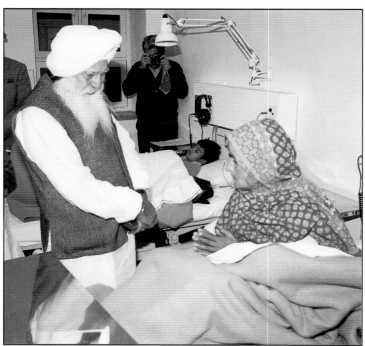

Visiting patients after the opening of the hospital.

The Sikanderpur hospital complex. 1999

In 1988, Maharaj Ji launched a new charitable hospital project in the village of Sikanderpur, near Sirsa in Haryana State. This area, having a strong association with Great Master, had a well-established tradition of service among the local people on which the project could be built. The 50-bed hospital was completed after Maharaj Ji passed away. The OPD department started functioning in August 1993, and the hospital became fully operational by 1994.

Giving instructions to Pehalwan at the hospital site.

Blessing parshad for sevadars during his last visit to the hospital site. March 1990

Master, before initiation I was scared of death.
After initiation I am scared of life.

One can understand a child who is scared of the dark.
The real tragedy is when we are afraid of the light.

CHAPTER FIVE

The Man for All Seasons

There is a story of a man walking along the beach, beside the mighty ocean, trying to figure out the meaning and purpose of the creation. As he walked, he noticed a young boy carrying buckets of water from the ocean to a small hole he had dug in the sand. Again and again the boy went back and forth from the ocean to the hole. Each time he tipped the water in, it was absorbed through the wet sand and disappeared. "What are you doing, child?" the man asked.

"I'm emptying the sea into this hole I've dug," replied the boy.

"Don't be silly," said the man. "That's impossible."

The boy was no ordinary boy. He knew what the man had been thinking as he walked, and he laughed a merry laugh. "If you think that's impossible, I'll tell you something equally silly. There's a man I know who's trying to understand life's mystery with his mind."

Trying to describe Maharaj Ji in words could be seen as an equally impossible task. One can certainly write about his activities; one can write about the events of his life; but to attempt to convey who he was, and claim to convey anything close to the truth, would be as foolish as the activities of both boy and man. The reader must therefore understand that these words are but a pointer to the reality—snippets of information and comments that are as the child's small buckets of water in relation to the sea.

The one word that comes to everyone's lips who knew Maharaj Ji is, without a shadow of doubt, 'love'. The personality of every Master would appear to be different in that one is remembered for his compassion, another for his kingliness, one for his humility, another for his dynamism. In the case of Maharaj Ji, it was love.

On either side of the word 'love' we have to place two companions: 'humility' and 'generosity'. Never did Maharaj Ji put himself forward, never did he take credit for anything, never did he see himself as other than a sevadar or friend. And as for generosity—he was generous of heart, generous with others' weaknesses, generous in praise and encouragement, generous with his time and generous with himself.

Whether as Master, son, husband, father or friend, he brought the same loving qualities to every relationship. He often used to say that there is far more joy in loving, in giving, and in serving than in being loved, receiving and being served— and he lived his life to demonstrate it.

In spite of his demanding schedule, he was for many people the best friend they ever had. How was it, one might wonder, that he achieved this extraordinary balance between his private and public activities?

Maharaj Ji lived the ideal he taught and by his life he demonstrated his secret. He used to often explain that the way to live is as an actor playing out his role on the stage. While fulfilling one's responsibilities in whatever situation one finds oneself, he advised, one should remember that the play of this life is not real. Our problems, he said, arise because our attachments cloud our thinking. We get over-involved in them, and we miss the real purpose of life—the opportunity to experience our spiritual nature.

Because he was teaching from experience, he was very pragmatic. Apart from the great 'remedy for all ills' of meditation, he said the trick for relaxation was to divert the mind. His personal diversion was photography. He would point out: "Mind also needs relaxation; your body also needs relaxation; you can attend to meditation much better." As he travelled across the world to carry his spiritual message, he pursued his hobby of photography. How many souls must he have touched with his attention focussed through his camera as he relaxed with his favourite recreation! Over the years he explored many different subjects, including tribal silver jewellery, monuments, temples and ancient buildings, wild life and, in his last years, roses by the thousands. And wherever he went, he photographed people.

He had an enormous zest and enthusiasm for life, which made him interested in everything. Historical, geographical, political or cultural—there was no fact too trivial for his attention. With his endless curiosity he'd keep his companions on their toes, invariably asking the one question for which no one present would have the answer.

Attached and inwardly directed to what was true, Maharaj Ji was both the most considerate, caring, and dependable person to be with, and he was also the most fun. Having truly surrendered his life to his Master, he had also surrendered his worries and cares. This made him light-hearted, humourous and carefree beyond imagination. Life was a non-stop celebration as this great star of God's theatre travelled across the face of the earth.

Nothing he did was by half measure. If he was host, he was the ultimate example of hospitality. If he was feeding guests, he would love to personally offer them all the things they would enjoy. If he was going to a particular place for photography, he would look into every detail of the journey. His stamina and his sustained interest amazed his companions. Whoever he was with—old or young, rich or poor, famous or unknown—and whatever he did—whether spending time with his mother, playing with his granchildren, photographing a flower, sitting talking with friends—he gave himself to the moment wholeheartedly.

Tanmarg, Kashmir. *L-R:* Janak Puri, Maharaj Ji, Louise Hilger, Ajit, Maharaj Ji's wife Harjeet. Summer 1952

It is a natural tendency of human beings to idealize anyone they love. It is this very tendency that leads, in the case of the mystics and saints, to miracles being ascribed to them, and their life history being romanticized after their death. Maharaj Ji used to explain that mystics come to the world as part of the creation, and as such, they live as normal human beings like anyone else. They have to have a father; they have to have a mother; they live as part of their culture and in keeping with their times.

Once someone asked Maharaj Ji to speak about his family and particularly his father, since not only was he Maharaj Ji's father but also the son of Great Master. Maharaj Ji commented: "What is there to know?" and went on to explain that biographical details were relevant only for generals and politicians: the saints' biography, he said, lies in their sangat and in their teachings, reflected through the sangat.

Gulmarg, Kashmir. Maharaj Ji, his father S. Harbans Singh (rear, centre), Louise (centre), Harjeet (right). 1952

Picnicking in Kashmir with *(L-R)* Maharaj Ji's father, R. C. Mehta, Janak Puri, Louise and Maharaj Ji. 1952

Within eighteen months of him becoming the Master, Maharaj Ji started to wear his beard down. One of the elder women of the family protested. As the beard and turban are symbols of honour and valour in the Sikh community, wearing one's beard loose is an action associated with older, retired people. Demonstrating to her that it made no difference whatsoever, he held his beard back up with his hand and said lightheartedly, "Who's 'let down' his beard?"

The wedding of Maharaj Ji's sister, Mohinder, in Sikanderpur. Maharaj Ji in front with his father to his left. 1952

With the bridegroom G. S. Dhillon, and Shoti.

With his nephew …

… on his first birthday with the parents and Shoti …

… at the turban-tying ceremony …

… the contented faces!

With Lakhi Dharmani. Mid '50s

With G. S. Dhillon and Colonel B. N. Sethi. 1956

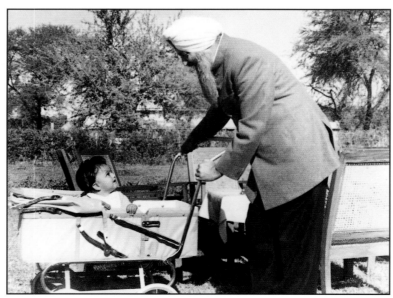

With Colonel Sethi's daughter.

With his father.

Sardar Harbans Singh, Maharaj Ji's father, was the third son of Great Master. More than anything else, he was remembered for his absolute obedience to Great Master. When he was told by him to send his boys—Maharaj Ji and Shoti—to Dera for their education, he never questioned Great Master's wish. He handed them over so fully into Great Master's trust that for many years the boys had no idea he was their father and thought of him as an uncle. His complete faith first in Great Master, and later, in his son, needs to be seen in the context of the practical difficulties those very close to a Master face in accepting his divine power and role. For someone to accept a close relation or friend as the Master, he or she has to be able to relinquish all self-interest in that relationship. Since, as Maharaj Ji so often pointed out, most of these relationships are based on some level of self-interest, it is a rare person who can make such sacrifice. It is a gift of grace, Maharaj Ji would say, to recognize a saint.

With his mother.

Beji, as Maharaj Ji's mother was known, was extremely hard-working and ran the family home in Sikanderpur. From when she married into the family and came to the farm as Great Master's daughter-in-law, up until late in Maharaj Ji's life, she took care of all the arrangements at Sikanderpur. This in itself was an enormous task: life in those days was tough in many ways, with very few of the amenities modern people take for granted.

Being the home of two Masters, it was for years a focal point both for the large extended family and for the entire sangat of that area. There was a constant stream of relatives, guests and sangat, and Beji would keep the kitchen running for hours on end. She made it a point to be personally involved with the up-bringing of all her children and she never sat idle. If she was not occupied in the kitchen or with the family, she would weave and make things for the home and for her daughters with her own hands.

Maharaj Ji with his wife, Nimmi and Rana.

With his family at Dera. *L-R:* Rana, Nimmi, Maharaj Ji, Harjeet, Cuckoo, Laddi (his niece), Pammi (his niece). 1957

With his family at Dera.

The true saint lives in the midst of other people.
He rises in the morning,
eats and sleeps when needed.
He buys and sells in the marketplace
just like everyone else.
He marries, has children,
and meets with his friends.
Yet never for an instant does he forget God.

Abu Saʻid

With his wife.

He was very tender with his mother. He was her son—always. Sitting in the kitchen, sitting with her on the floor, shelling peas in the courtyard of their home in Sikanderpur—with her, he could relax. He once commented that no one should suffer the misfortune of losing one's mother. As it transpired, it was his mother who had to suffer the pain of loss, as she outlived him by six years.

Relaxing with his mother.

Standing, L-R: Mohinder, Harjeet, Jogi, G. S. Dhillon, Maharaj Ji, P. S. Mann, Gurnam. *Middle row, L-R:* Maharaj Ji's mother, Tai Ji (Sardar Bachint Singh's wife), Bhua Ralli. *Front row, L-R:* Raj, Devi, Pammi. Minti in front.

Back row, L-R: Mrs Claire, Harjeet, Mrs R. N. Mehta, Diwan Sahib, Rao Sahib. *Middle row, L-R:* Monica, Maharaj Ji, Laddi, Pammi, Mr R. N. Mehta. *Front row, L-R:* Dicky, Guggu, Nimmi, Cookie.

Standing, L-R: Ram Kishan, Rao Sahib, Maharaj Ji, Shoti, Rajendra. *Seated, L-R:* Kamini (Ram Kishan's wife) with Manju, Harjeet, Maharaj Ji's mother-in-law, Abha (Rajendra's wife). *Front row, L-R:* Cuckoo, Nimmi, Rana.

393

In a boat on Powai Lake, Bombay, with Lakhi Dharmani, Nimmi and Laddi. 1957

With Ram Kishan and Nimmi in Bombay.

Maharaj Ji with Nimmi …

Talking once about the mind, he said:

*D*on't trust it. When my daughter was very small, her mother asked her, "Why are you not studying today?" She said, "Papa said in the satsang today, 'Never obey your mind.' And my mind says I should study, so I'm not going to." This is how we justify it!

395

In the Rishikesh hills.

Taking a break.

At Laxman Jhula, Hardwar, with Harjeet.

I recollect one incident in my life. Many years ago I went to Nainital—I was on my own and staying in some hotel, and there is a small gurdwara there. In the evening when I was out walking, I found about forty or fifty people sitting together and a priest was giving a discourse, so I sat down too. I was a little surprised at his interpretation of Guru Nanak's bani. They didn't know who I was, so after they all dispersed I talked to the priest and said this is not the right interpretation. I said Nam is something very different and I explained it to him.

He said: "That must be right. Next Sunday you come, and you give a talk."

So next Sunday I went there. There were about a hundred people and I spoke on Sant Mat, so to say, in the name of Guru Nanak. Everybody heard very attentively and even the priest was impressed and they were all very happy. Everything we were discussing was from the Adi Granth, nothing else. He thanked me and I left.

After four or five days, he again came to me with the idea that if I happened to be there, I should come the next Sunday too and give the lecture. I had been a little surprised when told that somebody wanted to see me because I didn't know anybody there and had gone there absolutely incognito. So I called him to my room. Fortunately or unfortunately, there were pictures of the Great Master and Sardar Bahadur Maharaj Ji on my side table. When he came, he sat there and just looked straight at the pictures. Then he looked at me and asked, "Are you Radha Soami?"

I said, "Yes."

Without any ceremony he walked out and all compliments were dashed from my previous lecture.

After that we often met on the road because there were hardly one or two roads where one could go for a walk. Yet he wouldn't even give a look of recognition—what to say of a greeting!

You see, people just get prejudiced. I was the same, my subject matter was the same, and I was not going to say anything different. But he just couldn't tolerate it.

With his sons, Rana and Cuckoo. 1960

With Cuckoo …

… with Rana.

A 'normal life' means to be good, disciplined citizens of our country, obedient and respectful to our parents, to do our job diligently and look after our family—to fulfil whatever responsibilities we have taken on our shoulders; and we have to be good friends. Then we have to make use of this human birth for that purpose which the Lord has bestowed this gift on us. That is a 'normal life'.

With his wife and children at Sikanderpur. 1964

In his last few years, Maharaj Ji spoke often about human values and the importance of the family. Was this because of the contrast between the life he himself had lived and the breakdown of the family unit he saw taking place across the world? He included his message in a Delhi satsang and in the book *Treasure Beyond Measure,* at which time he penned this handwritten note. He pointed out how modern civilization makes us unnatural—we become slaves to the very gadgets which are supposed to save us time and serve us—we suppress our grief and joy because we are so influenced by society, we are afraid to cry and we are afraid to laugh.

I am not against the modern
development of the present
civilization but at no cost
we should compromise with
the basic values of human
life. There should be leisure
for us. We should lead a
simple relaxed & tension
free life. There should be
a unity & peace in the family, respect
for the elders, and looking after
of the children. Our food
& environment should be
healthy. We should be sympathetic
& helpful to others. Our
development should lead
us to this direction.

Tea with guests in his dining room at Dera.

L-R: Lakhi Dharmani, Shoti, Maharaj Ji, Ram Kishan.

Listening to classical music at Mrs Bharat Ram's house in New Delhi.

Indore. 1964

With Harmohinder Ahuja and Janak Puri.

With Shanti Sethi.

With Dr and Mrs Garcha. 1962

*F*riendship means when you have a clean, clear
understanding with someone—he accepts you for
what you are, and you accept him for what he is,
and there is a clear understanding between both
of you. He wants to help you. You want to help
him. That is friendship. It is very rare.

With his wife and Louise at Dera. 1962

Opposite: In Dalhousie.

Writing to a friend —

*W*e always feel hurt from the people we love because we love them blindly and try to analyze every little thing that comes from them. If any little thing is lacking in them, we start feeling hurt. One shouldn't try to analyze anyone at all and should be happy in one's own love. Hurt comes when we expect something from the other person, and the more we expect the more we feel hurt. All of us have a particular part to play on this stage. Where love is, pain has to be there. Let me hope that you won't be affected by it and will remain happy in your own devotion.

Trekking in Kashmir, with R. C. Mehta, Madan and Usha Mehta, and Harjeet. 1965

Until the early seventies, Maharaj Ji was able to take fifteen or twenty days from his schedule to relax in the mountains with his family and friends. Later, in the eighties, he would comment how it was no longer possible— how his schedule kept him either at the Dera or on tour. "I used to go to the hills," he said, "but that is an old story now. For the last ten years I have hardly gone anywhere." He would go to Kashmir, or Dalhousie, mostly, as both were conveniently located in relation to the Dera. In Kashmir, he would stay with friends, or on a houseboat. They would go out trekking or spend long hours in the flat-bottom boats or *shikaras,* and dedicate entire days to photography. They were days of complete relaxation and recreation, and for his companions, they were days of endless delight.

In a houseboat on the Jhelum, Kashmir.

Maharaj Ji was on holiday. He entered the houseboat lounge looking dashing in his elegant churidar pyjama and kurta, and commented, "I feel like doing satsang." His companions enthusiastically responded, "Please sit on this divan, and talk to us of love." "What," he asked, "can I tell you of love? Do you know what love is? Love is a gift from the Lord." Lighthearted, and most beautifully, he had given the saints' teachings in a nutshell.

On a *shikara* (Kashmiri flat-bottomed boat) with R. C. Mehta.

412

In Kashmir with Chacha Ji (third from right), Harjeet, and the Mehta family.

With Madan, Usha and Harjeet.

In 1965, Maharaj Ji and his friends were high in the Kashmir mountains above Yusmarg and had camped for the night. Next morning, when they should have moved on to a higher camping site, Maharaj Ji, to everybody's surprise, instructed the porters and pony-wallahs to pack up and return immediately to Yusmarg. When they got back, they learnt that war had broken out between India and Pakistan. In fact, the mountain areas where they had been trekking were very unsafe.

Kashmir. 1965

To the perfectly humble there is nothing lacking, spiritual or physical. For they have God, in whom is all abundance, and whoever has him—as this book keeps on saying—needs nothing else in this life.
Cloud of Unknowing

Visiting his daughter in Dalhousie.

Group picture of his daughter's college visit to the Dera.

With the family in Ranchi. Mid '60s

With his daughter.

In Pahalgam, Kashmir. 1964

419

On a boat on the Arabian Sea, Bombay. 1966

Photography at the Ajanta Caves with Bea Jauncey. 1966

Photographing the Jain temples at Ranakpur, Rajasthan. 1967

The Lord does not stay in these temples of brick and mortar that we make for his residence. He is right within your body; but, says Christ, you do not bother to seek him in your body. You worship the Father in these man-made temples. You do not care for the temple that the Lord has given you and in which he resides. The human body is called the temple of the living God, because in this temple and in no other can we live with God and become God.

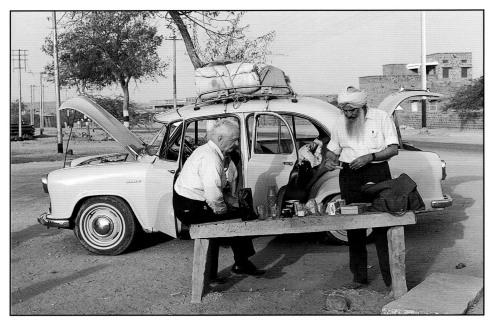
A roadside picnic with Dr Stone and Madan Mehta near Pokhran, Rajasthan.

Coffee break with Dr Stone in Rajasthan.

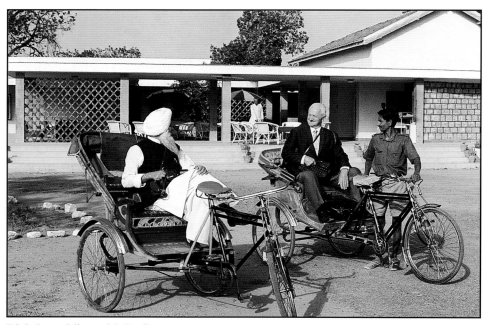
Rickshaw riding with Dr Stone.

Maharaj Ji was at home everywhere. On the ground, the floor or a comfortable chair, in a palace, a house or a ruin, in the desert or snow, he was comfortable and relaxed. "Life itself is very simple," he used to say. "And our needs are very simple in this creation. We complicate our needs by our requirements. We create problems at every step and then we try to solve them."

In Ishi Mehta's vintage car, Srinagar, Kashmir.

Rajasthan. 1971

Nepal. 1968

*I*f your Master is in all the activities of your daily life,
if you don't forget him at any moment, then everything
is submission to him—everything is him.

With Nimmi, his wife and Col. B.N. Sethi in Nepal. 1968

Nepal. 1968

Nepal. 1968

With Harjeet and Nimmi in Chandigarh. 1969

With R. C. Mehta's family and Sam Busa in Gulmarg, Kashmir.

With Ken and Cami Moss and Mrs R. N. Mehta above Manali.

With Harjeet in Manali. 1970

Whenever he travelled on holiday, like a child he was curious about everything. The range of his knowledge and his interest in detail was phenomenal.

Rajasthan.

Jaipur airport lounge. (Neil Armstrong holding the newspaper.)

Rajasthan.

As a photographer, Maharaj Ji went through several distinct phases. He was first interested in people, faces, landscapes, architectural shots and old monuments with details of their carvings and sculptures. Then came the silver jewellery phase, shot on trips to Rajasthan and indoors, at his home. This was followed by a wild life phase—with photographic safaris to various national parks in central India and Rajasthan. Finally came the flowers. Initially, he shot flowers as and where they were. This put a lot of strain on his back, so he devised a method where a rose would be fixed to the top of an iron rod fixed into the ground. Life became easier. Now he could concentrate on the technical details to get the best of shots. Once the film was processed, he would like nothing better than to call a few friends and enjoy viewing the slides with them in his sitting room. His enthusiasm was boundless.

At the Ellora caves with Cami Moss.

Maharaj Ji with Chatru.

In his later years, wherever Maharaj Ji went, Chatru, his personal attendant, could be seen nearby. Maharaj Ji always liked to be prepared to shoot in colour, black and white, or movie, depending on the situation. Chatru, like a surgeon's assistant, would be there, ready to give him the specific lens, camera, or film, in immediate response to Maharaj Ji's outstretched hand.

434

435

He always wore his watch on the inside of his wrist. When asked why, he commented that it was easier to keep an eye on the time that way. Whether giving satsang, holding a meeting, or attending to personal or family work, he was punctual to the minute. Day after day, through the years, one could set one's watch according to the moment he arrived.

*O*nly attachment can create detachment.
Detachment never creates attachment in anybody.

If anybody slanders you or abuses you—don't accept it. It will go back to him. If you don't accept a parcel, the postman will take it back.

This path is the easiest to understand, the easiest to follow, and the hardest to achieve.

With nothing in our pocket and the Father with us—this is the best grace we can have from the Father.

We should not curse the darkness, we should light the candle. Automatically it will help to eliminate the darkness.

If you want Him to give cloak to your weaknesses, then you should also not expose others weaknesses.

In Sant Mat, there are no failures—because you are trying to follow it. So even if we lose in this battle of love, we still win.

Nimmi's wedding. *L-R:* Shoti, Nimmi, Pammi, Maharaj Ji. 1970

The Pisawa family (Maharaj Ji's in-laws) at Nimmi's wedding.

Nimmi's wedding reception. *Standing, L-R:* Guddu, Rana, Rajendra Singh, Cuckoo. *Seated, L-R:* Pammi's younger brother Manu, Pammi, Harjeet, Nimmi, Maharaj Ji, Laddi, Bambi.

The fond father.

With Bhai Mohan Singh, Nimmi's father-in-law.

Maharaj Ji 'occupying' himself moments after Nimmi's *doli* (when the bride leaves her parents' home).

With Shoti.

With Shoti and his mother. 1974

With Cuckoo and Rana. 1971

With Nimmi and Laddi.

1984

Maharaj Ji often expressed his concern at the ever-deteriorating commitment he witnessed to the institution of marriage. Talking about the many letters he received regarding marital problems, he once said to the Westerners: "Now I've stopped writing anything at all, because my advice hardly makes any difference to anybody." In the winter of 1989, however, he made the question of human values, and particularly marriage, one of his main themes. It was a central part of his last guidance to his English-speaking sangat. He quoted Sardar Bahadur Ji's words: "Marriage is marriage and that is the solution," and gave the simple instruction: "You should both get to know each other ... sit down and try to find out how to help each other." When commenting on children being raised by a single parent, he said that children need both—the father for security, and the mother for warmth.

Laddi's wedding. February 1965

Cuckoo's wedding. January 1975

Rana's wedding. April 1975

At Cuckoo's engagement.

Bhai Mohan Singh and Maharaj Ji dancing at Cuckoo's wedding.

With family members at Cuckoo's engagement.

O Nanak, meeting the true Master, one learns the perfect way to live.
Then laughing, playing, dressing or eating, while living in Maya, one finds liberation.

Adi Granth

Sehra bandi at Cuckoo's wedding.

Seeing that many people in the West were losing faith in the value of the institution of marriage, he would sometimes say lightheartedly that it was risky to ask Westerners about their spouses, in case they should turn around and ask, 'Which one?' On a more serious note, he would explain that the marriage vow is necessary to protect a relationship. "If you want the shoe to stay on," he would say, "you have to tie the lace."

Rana's wedding. *L-R:* Shoti, Maharaj Ji, Rana, Cuckoo, Dicky …

… with *(L-R)* Cuckoo, Harjeet, Nimmi, Bela, Rana, Pammi …

… with Cuckoo and Rana.

With his new daugher-in-law Sadhana, and Rana.

The happy parents.

Father and daughter.

Cuckoo's wedding. A traditional game played by the newly married couple.

His laughter was spontaneous, vibrant, joyful and infectious. He would catch his lower lip in his teeth as though this were the only way he could stop himself laughing too much. Were he not himself to limit it, one felt his merriment might shake the whole world.

456

1975

*E*xcept humans, nobody laughs. I don't think you would have ever seen a bird laughing, or a dog laughing, or an animal laughing! They may smile, but you have not seen them laughing. This privilege is only given to humans. If we want to remain humans, humour has to be there just to relax. But we have so much association with the past species, we find it very hard to laugh.

With R. C. Mehta. 1972

With Madan and Dishi Mehta.

With Tejindra Khanna. 1988

With *(L-R)* Chacha Ji's wife, A. N. Mehta, Chacha Ji and R. N. Mehta.

With Sheila Bharat Ram and Janak Puri.

With Dr Stone. December 27, 1973

459

The more a man is at one within himself and becomes single in heart, the more he understands higher things without labour; for he receives the light of understanding from above.

Thomas à Kempis

With Pammi, his son-in-law.

With Bela and Sadhana, his daughters-in-law.

462

With the three children, his son-in-law, daughters-in-law and his first four grandchildren.

With his grandchildren

... traditional occasions: naming ceremonies and turban-tying of the grandchildren ...

In front of the ancestral home in Sikanderpur. 1987

With his niece Laddi and her sons.

With his four sisters, brother and mother.

With Bibi Ralli. 1976

Maharaj Ji had been closely associated with Bibi Ralli since his earliest childhood and she was one of his closest confidantes. A completely dedicated soul, she had lived her entire life at the Dera and served the Great Master from youth. Maharaj Ji described her once as the "soul of this whole colony", and explained how much she had always cared about the Dera. He spoke of her as a "wonderful, wonderful lady" who, inspite of a slight attack of paralysis, was active, happy and content.

With Dr Dhillon and his mother.

With his mother. 1986

Explaining one's responsibilities towards one's elderly relatives, Maharaj Ji used to tell a story in the English meetings: In large Indian homes there is often a gatehouse—an independent accomodation built into the main courtyard entrance. Several generations would typically live together, and as the younger generation would take over the responsibilities of the family, the older generation would shift from the main house to the gatehouse. So, one very cold winter's day, the grand-father of the family asked his grandson to fetch him a blanket. The young boy went to his father. "It's very cold," said the boy to his father, "and grandfather finds it chilly in the gatehouse. He wants a blanket to keep himself warm."

His father replied, "There is an old blanket in the stable, which the horses use. You can give it to him."

The son fetched the blanket, cut it into two pieces, gave half to the grandfa-ther and brought the other half back.

"There was no need to cut it in two," said his father. "I told you simply to give him the blanket."

"Well," said his son, "This half I have kept for you, for when you get old."

Maharaj Ji was very clear. "It is our responsibility to look after our elders, and we should take care of them in every way."

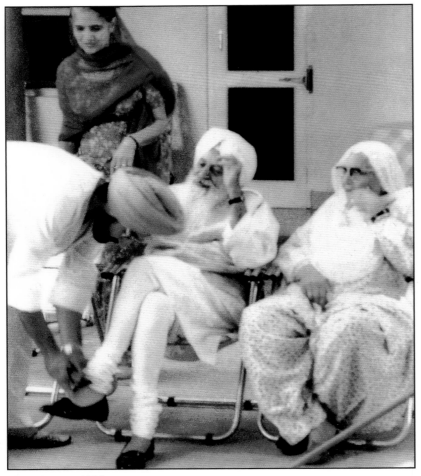

Sikanderpur. 1989

That exalted status is yours,
When I bow my head before you;
Yet this head I bow
Is but a gift from you to me.
Far more than my destiny allows
From your gracious hands I receive;
Yet even my destiny
Is but a gift from you to me.

Yaha rootba tere dar ko
mere sir se milaa hai,
Haalaanki yahee sir bhee mujhe
tere dar se milaa hai.
Miltaa hai tere dar se,
mukardar se bhee zyaadaa.
Haalaanki yaha mukardar bhee
tere dar se milaa hai.

Anonymous Urdu couplets

With the extended family. 1988

474

Rajasthan. 1976

Maharaj Ji loved Rajasthan. Its rural life was still largely unspoilt, and the people lived by the rhythms and traditions they had known for centuries. Most of the faces Maharaj Ji photographed there were villagers, untouched by the complications and affectations of modern urban life. They were a people confident and clear in themselves, and they had that curiosity which is natural to most living creatures. As he looked at them through his lens, they too looked straight at him.

With Nimmi, dressed in tribal silver jewellery.

Roadside tea break with Chacha Ji and E. R. Naidu (standing behind him).

It was the eighties, and he was travelling by road in North India when the car had two punctures, one after the other. They had no option but to look for a roadside workshop where they could get one puncture, at least, re-paired. They pulled over to the first suitable place, and started the work. An enthusiastic young mechanic took on the task and Maharaj Ji stayed inside the car so as not to attract any attention. While waiting, someone in the party noticed Maharaj Ji's picture on the wall of the workshop. Once the job was complete, he asked the mechanic whose photo it was. "That is the photograph of my parents' Master," the boy replied with pride in his voice. Maharaj Ji was told, and he rolled down his window so the boy could see who was inside. The boy literally jumped for joy!

Wherein lies the perfection of a man? In giving yourself over with all your heart to the divine will, not seeking your own things either great or small, in time or in eternity. Thus will you keep an even countenance—in thanksgiving, amidst prosperity and adversity—weighing all things with an equal balance.

Thomas à Kempis

At Mandu, Madhya Pradesh, with *(clockwise, starting centre front)* V. K. Sethi, T. K. Sethi, Usha Mehta, R. N. Mehta, Mrs Mehta, Harjeet, Maharaj Ji, Ken Moss, Pammi, with Sheila Bharat Ram in the centre of the group. 1980

With the Sethis, Mosses, Mehtas, Sheila Bharat Ram, and his family in Indore, Madhya Pradesh. 1980

Travelling by train during the same trip. 1980

With Ken and Cami Moss at the Kumbh Mela, Ujjain.

Ken and Cami Moss were to accompany Maharaj Ji to the Kumbh Mela. Maharaj Ji loved good-natured practical jokes and on this occasion he decided that Cami would dress as a sadhu. He had a tailor make special saffron coloured robes for her and to complete the effect, Cami parted her hair in the centre and wore garlands around her neck.

When they entered the fair, Maharaj Ji, the photographer, acted the perfect tourist, enjoying the sights and taking pictures. As they moved about, people soon started bowing at Cami's feet.

Cami said to Maharaj Ji, "How can you let them bow at my feet? I'm not a real sadhu."

Maharaj Ji laughed. "The real sadhus aren't any better than you," he said.

The irony was that everyone bowed to Cami because she was wearing saffron robes, but no one recognized Maharaj Ji because he was dressed in ordinary clothes.

Very rarely did Maharaj Ji get a chance to be on his own. In a letter written to a friend, when on holiday in Bangalore during the early 1970s, he remarked:

I love this solitude and peace, and not being haunted by any visitors. Life is so simple and beautiful to live, provided one can rise above human failings. They always keep you entangled in the net of worry and misery.

Whatever has to happen has already happened, and we mortals are just helpless spectators. If we can just withdraw this 'self', then only can we enjoy this drama of life.

Relaxing in Manali, with the Mehtas and Teji Khanna. 1981

*W*e should be serious about following Sant Mat, but that doesn't mean that we should disregard the cheerful side of life altogether. Rather, we should feel more relaxed because we are following the path.

Manali. 1981

Shekhavati. 1987

With *(L-R)* Madan Gopal Singh, Madan Mehta, Janak Gorwaney and Harjeet in Shekhavati.

The Sufi Master, while being gracious to all the disciples, could not conceal his preference for those who lived in the 'world'—the married, the merchants, the farmers—over those who lived in the monastery. When he was confronted about this he said, "Spirituality practised in the state of activity is incomparably superior to that practised in the state of withdrawal."

486

Maharaj Ji's photo was about to be taken when one of the party seemed concerned. He took Maharaj Ji aside and spoke something to him confidentially. What he had noticed, in fact, was that there was a tiny mark on Maharaj Ji's kurta. Maybe it would come in the photo, he thought, and it wouldn't look nice. Maharaj Ji threw his head back and gave one of those wonderful earth-shaking laughs of his. "Such a vast expanse of white," he said, "and you're concerned for such an insignificant speck of dirt!"

Coffee break at Jaigarh fort, Rajasthan. 1987

Taking a break in the shade of a derelict house in Rajasthan.

With Janak Gorwaney in Rajasthan. 1987

Photographing from Jaigarh fort, Rajasthan.

Maharaj Ji would put himself into all sorts of precarious and uncomfortable situations to get a good picture. Sometimes, this made it awkward for his companions. Should they hold him round the middle so he wouldn't fall—or just hold tight to the two corners of his kurta? Maharaj Ji himself said that to be a good photographer, one should expect to have at least a few falls. This he offered with a smile as consolation to one of his companions who had fallen into a muddy pond when photographing a group of camels that had come to drink. The fun of that incident was that the camels walked in a single-file line across Maharaj Ji's path, then regrouped themselves, faced him, and all stood in a row looking at him! A perfect group shot!

With *(L-R):* the Game Warden, Faith Singh and her daughter, Madan Gopal Singh, John Singh and Madan Mehta in Ranthambhore National Park. 1987

During one trip, when Maharaj Ji and his party arrived in the park, everyone was greatly impressed by an enormous banyan tree. They spent a delightful fifteen minutes or so fooling around, with everyone photographing everyone among its aerial roots and branches. Maharaj Ji, at the beginning of this trip, had cautioned them to photograph only what they were supposed to. Though he had not specified what "supposed to" meant, they assumed it meant not to focus too much on Maharaj Ji. So here, sitting on the great branch of the banyan, one of the party had his video on his lap, with the cap off, camera running, while Maharaj Ji was taking his own photograph of the group. "Who's photographing whom?" he said, clearly recognizing what was going on. They all laughed.

Later during the trip, when Maharaj Ji was relaxing, the same person was discreetly photographing Maharaj Ji's reflection in a great brass pot near his chair. "Why photograph the reflection when the real thing is before you?" Maharaj Ji asked. And then philosophically he added, "How we spend our time chasing after shadows and reflections!"

Morning break in Bundi, Rajasthan.

Dinner at Samode Palace, Rajasthan. 1987

Near the Jaipur–Samode road in Rajasthan. 1987

Relaxing on a farmer's string bed, Maharaj Ji commented to his companions, "I am a farmer—you couldn't have found a better place: water, trees and a bed." That night at dinner he said it was the first time since the '40s that he had got the opportunity of resting under a tree. He said that when he was practising law he sometimes used to take his books and rest under the trees at his farm.

In Kanha National Park. 1987

With Pammi and Madan Mehta photographing spiderwebs.

Maharaj Ji used to say that the secret of a happy life lies in the way one adjusts to it—that if one can't change the events of life, one can at least meet them with a relaxed and carefree attitude. They were out looking for tiger, but meanwhile he found plenty of interesting subjects for his photography, including an enormous dew-hung spider's web. As for the tiger, his comment was: "If we see one—very good. If we don't, well, that's his destiny."

Looking for tigers in Kanha.

Photographing a tiger in Ranthambore National Park. 1988

Photograph taken by Maharaj Ji.

With John and Faith Singh and their daughter, on the road to Alwar, Rajasthan. 1988

When travelling on holiday, Maharaj Ji would always leave very early, and carry morning snacks and usually a picnic lunch with him. By nine in the morning he would be ready for a coffee break when he would drink one cup of coffee and eat something. On one occasion, making a comment that included the Punjabi word *niyyat*, he directed Chatru to bring him a second cup—an action which seemed untypical of him. On being asked what he had meant, he explained: "The stomach is full, but the desire still remains." Someone then asked, "Is this where all our problems originate, we humans, that we are never content?" He laughed and said, "Yes, but we shouldn't worry about these little things. We have come so far in spite of this *niyyat.*"

Beas. 1988

In the last years of his life, with his travels limited by security constraints and his schedule leaving him so little time, he concentrated on photographing flowers. In particular, he loved to photograph roses and took slides of them in thousands. Sometimes he would prepare the roses for the picture, taking a dropper and placing small beads of water into their petals. Once, when he was giving a slide show, someone asked him if that was really how they looked. He explained: "First I dress them up in all their finery. And then I capture them in my lens." When his mother asked him why he took so many pictures of flowers, he told her, somewhat philosophically, "They don't ask anything of me—and they always smile."

499

To see a world in a grain of sand
And a heaven in a wildflower,
Hold infinity in the palm of your hand
And eternity in an hour.

William Blake

Rajasthan, 1989

Maharaj Ji always had a way of looking on the bright side of life, no matter what the circumstances. Rajasthan is a hot desert state, and on one occasion some of his group had chosen to sleep on the roof terrace because of the heat. During the night, a dust storm blew up and their mosquito nets collapsed around them, causing everyone to shift beds and bedding back indoors. One person, however, unperturbed by all the commotion, slept on through the night in a tangle of bamboo poles and mosquito netting. This brought about a conversation the following morning during which Maharaj Ji commented that "a man truly at peace with himself could sleep on the edge of a sword." Someone complained that as a result of the disturbed sleep he felt "miserable". Maharaj Ji laughed and said he shouldn't feel miserable: the morning air was pleasant and they'd passed a good night. "I slept sound," was another comment, "to the sound of mosquitoes," to which Maharaj Ji responded with a mischievous smile: "My sound was much better."

His last Rajasthan trip in March 1989, with his family, Cami and Madan Gopal Singh.

Picnic lunch.

He didn't eat much himself, but he loved to feed others, to give and share with them whatever they especially liked. His manner was bountiful—you could say abundance was truly his measure—and just as he himself enjoyed life, he showered everyone around him with the same sense of enjoyment.

Sunset in Jaisalmer. *L-R:* Bela, Maharaj Ji, Nimmi, Sadhana, Madan Gopal Singh, Cami and Laddi.

On the sand dunes of the Thar desert near Jaisalmer. March 1989

At White Tiger Forest Lodge, Bhandavgarh, Madhya Pradesh. *Standing in front:* T. K. Sethi's three sons and Madan Gopal Singh. *Back, L-R:* Harmohinder Ahuja, B. K. Sethi, Tata Sethi, T. K. Sethi, Chatru. February 1990

With Madan Gopal Singh …

… T. K. Sethi and B. K. Sethi …

… security sevadars …

… the drivers, cooks and attendants.

Maharaj Ji had himself photographed in a group with all the drivers, cooks, attendants, security personnel—all who had served him during the trip. He took care to see that each one of them got a copy of the photograph—for them it was a momento of a lifetime. Wherever he went, everyone concerned felt his personal touch, irrespective of how they were placed in life. He was particular to say a word of appreciation and thanks to any staff who attended on him, and took personal care to see all were comfortably lodged and properly fed.

Opposite: Khajuraho. February 1990

511

Inspite of his kingly impression, when one looked carefully at his lovely face and tender, compassionate eyes, one saw a saint. Such a face you would never have seen before—a face combining age, power and majesty with beauty, serenity and tenderness.

Have patience! In time, even grass becomes milk.

CHAPTER SIX

Legacy of Love

The first hint of the momentous event that was to come in 1990 was in the previous year when Maharaj Ji fell ill. In April 1989, for the first time ever, he cancelled a scheduled Delhi satsang programme. On an earlier occasion, too, he had been very unwell, yet the satsang programme had gone ahead. At that time he had a racking cough that made it impossible for him to speak. But when those close to him suggested the programme be cancelled, he said that it was for Great Master to take his work from him as he pleased. For the duration of the satsang his cough subsided. The moment he was off the stage, it struck back with the same troubling and exhausting frequency as before.

Talking about the cancelled April programme in November 1989, he dismissed all concerns saying: "Colds and other aches and pains are just a normal function of the body. I run too fast for them to cooperate. They try to pull me back. I am not suffering, don't worry about it."

In hindsight, however, it seemed to some of his closest companions and disciples that he knew he was going. In many different ways, he gave signs that would only be recognized as such after he had gone.

First of all, and most significantly, he had released the book *Treasure Beyond Measure* just weeks before he left. No book had been rushed through the press so quickly. All who worked on it through the previous year had commented on the sense of urgency that accompanied it through authorship, editing and printing. Here, for the first time, was a book that revealed the private face of Maharaj Ji to the entire sangat. It spoke of what it felt like to be appointed a Master; and of how difficult he had found the transition in the first few years. It showed how much strength he had drawn from the loving support of the sangat, and from his family and friends. It spoke about what it meant to live in the Lord's will.

He took a personal interest in having every family member and friend read the book. It put the record straight and in the open about the difficulties a successor might face in his situation. Many who were close to Maharaj Ji could not understand at the time why he should choose to publish such a book. After June 1, it became eminently clear. More than any other single action, this revelation of Maharaj Ji, the private person, paved the way for his successor.

There were many other pointers to his decision to go, but as long as his physical presence was there, no one saw them in that light. In March '89 he had called together all his closest family members to join him on what was to be his last holiday with the family. He squeezed those days into his schedule, driving a non-stop ten-hour journey back to Delhi to present himself to the overseas sangat who were awaiting him there, since the Punjab had not yet been opened to foreigners. In March 1990, he took away all the spare sets of clothes he kept at his farm in Sikanderpur and at Pusa Road, Delhi, saying he would not need them there anymore. In mid-May, 1990, he sent Madan Mehta, his close associate and friend in all his photographic activities, the note reproduced later in this book, saying categorically that there would be no more pictures. But as long as he was there, few could imagine the unthinkable. A letter written by a Western satsangi during the December 1989 session of evening meetings noted the following:

Master seemed very old and tired today. I began to wonder for how long he will be with us. He seemed like a frail translucent vessel containing the water of life: waves of light are radiating from within him... It seemed like a foretaste of farewell. The body is old and he will leave us. The thought of his leaving just increases our love. Everything is love in one way or another.

Someone remarked to him that he was afraid one day soon we would all be in deep trouble because he would be leaving us. Master replied without hesitation, "No, no one will be in trouble." And he spoke of Jesus' words about sending the comforter: "Worship of the spirit is the only real worship. This is the only worship which pleases the Lord. The body is not Shabd. Shabd is the real Master. We should hang on to the Shabd."

When asked what he missed about the old Dera, Maharaj Ji replied, "Well, I definitely miss my own Master," and at that moment he began to cry. "Every brick, every stone reminds us of him," he said. We were all deeply moved by the sight of his love.

When asked a few days later how he could be sad about his Master's absence when he doubtless was able to see him within, he said that the physical form of the Master is equally important as the inner form.

Maharaj Ji was undoubtedly preparing the sangat for his departure, and after he left, these many small indicators consoled the sangat. They affirmed that just as he had been in control of his life, so he was of his death. In that last winter session with the foreigners, someone had marvelled how it was that Maharaj Ji kept on and on with such a gruelling schedule. He replied that it was no effort for him—swimming against the current, he said, is always strenuous, but to swim with the flow, that involves no effort at all. He then went on to say that he was

"simply floating along with the tide of the sangat's love".

His words encapsulated his life. He had aligned himself perfectly with the supreme will. There was no separation between the two.

Thanks — Inspite of me, I am still breathing in His Service.
Charan Singh

[handwritten] Man's life does not commence in the womb and never ends in the grave.

Man's life does not commence in the womb and never ends in the grave.

[handwritten] Love is a great precious treasure, it is God's gift to sensitive and great spirits.

Love is a precious treasure, it is God's gift to sensitive and great spirits.

[handwritten] Congratulations! May you grow & grow to enjoy The Everlasting Life. Love, Charan Singh

Congratulations! May you grow & grow to enjoy the Everlasting Life.
Love, Charan Singh

When we attend a saint's satsang, we come to know what is real. We learn that we will gain nothing from external practices, that the Lord lives within us and it is there we must search for him by turning within. By keeping the company of saints, true love for the Lord and the longing to find him will be awakened within us.

∼

Why the Master? We contemplate on the form of the Master because his real form is Shabd, he is the Word made flesh, and by contemplating on his form we are getting attached to the Shabd inside, to the audible life stream of which the Master is the embodiment.

The saints and mystics are waves of the ocean of the true Shabd. They come into the world, bear witness to the Shabd and preach the Shabd. Then they take us with them and merge back into the ocean of the Shabd.

Soami Ji (1818–1878)

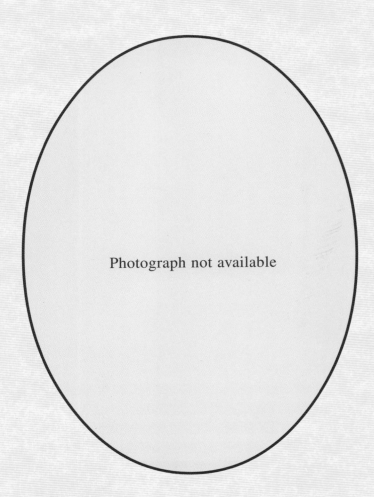

Baba Jaimal Singh (1839–1903)

Maharaj Sawan Singh (1858–1948)

Sardar Bahadur Jagat Singh (1884–1951)

Maharaj Charan Singh (1916–1990)   Baba Gurinder Singh (1954–

*L*ove means obedience. Love means submission.
Love means losing your identity to become another being.
That is love.

Sardar Bahadur Jagat Singh arriving for his *dastarbandi* (turban-tying) ceremony. April 13, 1948

Dastarbandi of Maharaj Charan Singh. November 4, 1951

This body has to be left here by both disciple and Master. The soul of a disciple will never be abandoned by the Shabd, once it has been inwardly linked to it through the Master. Drawn by the Shabd, it will definitely merge in the Lord. Thus, the Shabd is the real Master, and our soul is the real disciple.

When Maharaj Ji returned from the Delhi satsang in March 1990, it was observed that he did not appear interested in what was happening around him. When asked what the matter was, he replied, "Nothing interests me and nothing holds me here. My work is done."

The May bhandara came with all its hectic activities. Maharaj Ji gave the satsangs on May 24, 25, 26 and 27. It was noticed by everyone that these satsangs, particularly the last, were marked by an extraordinary degree of fluency of speech and eloquence of appeal. On May 26, he took a shabd by Soami Ji: *Dham apne chalo bhai,* "O brother, turn thou homeward now." This shabd, like no other, reminds the sangat of the brief nature of life on earth.

On the morning of Sunday, May 27, Maharaj Ji felt cardiac pain, which later in the afternoon became quite severe. He didn't consult the doctors lest they should ask him to cancel the satsang, which would have disappointed the huge gathering numbering over 300,000 people. All through the eighty minutes of the satsang he took care to see that his voice, gestures and expression would not betray the real state of his health. The entire satsang was delivered in his usual mellifluous but forceful voice. To many, he looked unusually radiant.

This was the last occasion on which the sangat saw him, yet little did anyone realize that he had decided to leave this world. His illness, as it became clear later, was just an excuse he had found to divert those around him. The doctor examined him that evening and requested him to take complete rest.

On Tuesday, May 29, Maharaj Ji was not well enough to make his daily visit to his mother. She herself had not been keeping good health and was unable to go upstairs to visit him. On Wednesday, May 30, he requested that she be brought to him. With three of his four sisters also present, he talked with her in a leisurely manner about the small and personal matters they always shared. He then took her hand and placed it for some minutes upon his head—the blessings of a mother to her son—and took her leave. She never saw him again.

On the Wednesday he also called his other close family members and gave personal and specific guidance to each. Even at this juncture his illness appeared to most people as a trouble that would soon pass. He asked his son to bring some of his personal funds to his room, and then to each and every one who had been employed in his household he handed a gift of money. Their tears could not be contained—yet Maharaj Ji was calm and reassuring to all. To each of the medical attendants and technicians who were looking after him he gave a small memento, and to Dr Joshi he gave a clock that was not working at the time. Ironically, the time showing on the clock was the exact time that Maharaj Ji left his mortal coil two days later.

Unbeknown to the family, Maharaj Ji also called the Dera Secretary, Shri S. L. Sondhi, and some other senior satsangis. What he said came as a terrible shock to them. He dictated his will, appointing Gurinder Singh Dhillon, son of Sardar Gurmukh Singh Dhillon of Moga, as his spiritual successor, entrusting him with the power and authority to give satsangs and initiate seekers, and appointed him as the Patron of the Radha Soami Satsang Beas Society and the Maharaj Jagat Singh Medical Relief Society Beas. After the draft was complete, Maharaj Ji put on his reading glasses and went through it carefully. He then had it read out to the witnesses.

On May 31, he commented to Dr Joshi, "This body is no longer fit for seva, so what is the point of keeping it?" Dr Joshi protested and said that his illness might be a temporary phase, that he should be able to recover and, in course of time, function normally. In response to questions from family members, Dr Joshi consistently replied that clinically there was no reason why Maharaj Ji should not recover. He had asked Maharaj Ji earlier in the week whether he would like to be shifted to the hospital or whether they should seek the additional help of a specialist. Maharaj Ji had replied firmly that he would stay at his home and that he was well satisfied with the medical arrangements. He was, at every moment, clearly in control of all that was happening to him. When Dr Joshi reminded him of his promise that he would be all right, Maharaj Ji replied, "Everything is happening according to the will of the Lord."

When, around midday on June 1, he finally left his body, it was with the same simplicity that he had lived. He requested those attending to him to help him lie down—he said he wanted to rest. Once he was comfortable, he asked that they cover him with a sheet, turn out the light, and leave the room. He had done what he had to do. His work was complete. The moment they reached the adjoining room, the line on the heart monitor went flat and the alarms went off. Beloved, beautiful and wondrous being, he had left his physical body—he had merged with the Shabd.

His mortal frame was brought for darshan to the satsang compound and placed on a specially prepared reclining dais in front of the platform from where he had delivered satsangs for the last several decades. On June 2, in the early hours of the morning, thousands filed past the bier—about 1,250,000 people reached the Dera to have a last look at their beloved Master. There he was, beautiful and serene as ever, the magnificent white beard, the same benign expression of tranquillity on his face, and the familiar divine glow, which had won the hearts of friends and foes alike. It was the start of a new beginning: the light had merged, but another had been lit.

We are depressed, sorrowfully we sigh, weep,
   we will always remember your love.
You were the throne-keeper in all the realms,
   sovereigns and magnates reverenced you.
Lovely and kind was your nature,
   mild your talk that never showed bitter anger.

Great Giant, strong in patience,
   you tolerated everybody, you were renowned for it.
Righteous, innocent, merciful, bountiful,
   generous, compassionate, kind Father,
   who made happy the oppressed;
You who saved numberless souls from distress
   and guided them to their Home.
Strong, good, powerful one, who like all apostles,
   buddhas and gods, have now gone to your throne.
To you I pay homage,
   I, the smallest of your sons, who has been left an orphan
   and an exile by you, dear Father.

Come hither, let us write a letter to the beneficent King of Light.
From him we will beg: forgive our sins!

                Part of a eulogy first given on the death of Mar Zako,
                a successor to the third-century Iranian mystic, Mani.

The present Master with Shoti before the *dastarbandi*. 1990

A slave always dances to the tune of his Master. He doesn't exert his own will because he has no will of his own. He has merged his will into the will of his Master. He has committed himself to obey his Master. So we become his slave. We want to live in his will.

DECEMBER 12, 1916 – JUNE 1, 1990, man and Master in one, Maharaj Ji danced the dance of life magnificently, selflessly, serenely, flawlessly. In laying down his mortal frame—fearless, calm, reassuring, radiant and re-splendent—he affirmed his message of the eternal Shabd, of love; and he showed how this brief act upon creation's stage should end.

Is it a wonder then, when we think of him or when life brings his image before us, that we miss his physical presence? As Hafiz so poignantly put it:

> His face, moon of form, we beheld not to our fill;
>   and he departed.
> In the rose garden of union with him, we moved not;
>   and he departed.
> On his face, we fully cast not our glance;
>   and he departed.
> Alas! For bidding him farewell, we arrived not;
>   and he departed.

It is his legacy of love, his most precious gift to us, that holds us on the path he placed us on. He always said, "Love is within you, and is not to be found anywhere outside." The love and recognition that we seek from the body Master is already there within us. "Our souls are already in love with the Lord," he would say. His gifts can be had, here and now, at the eye centre. We only have to believe and look.

Consummate friend and inseparable, divine companion, he is both the life-giving Shabd that sustains us, and he is his successor, with us still on the physical plane. Our Master is at all times giving us his immeasurable protection. It is a great, good fortune to meet a perfect saint such as he in one's lifetime. When we view it from the standpoint of total existence, life after life and aeon upon aeon, such good fortune cannot be conceived. We can only marvel that any being can be so blessed.

533

Charan Singh
19.10.57.

534

*T*ry to find someone who really belongs to us,
and to whom we can really belong—forever.

536

Pray! you grow & grow
to become one with
Him
                Love
                Charal
                24.1.90

The current of love from the one God is flowing through
the entire universe. What do you think when you look at the
face of a man? Look at him carefully. He is not a man but
a current of love, the essence of God, which permeates him.

Rumi

Madan.

This film is definitely the last. I have even taken out the cells from the camera. Thanks, love Chip

In the last years, whenever Maharaj Ji would send a roll of film to Madan for developing, he would wrap it in a handwritten note—he always wanted some comment on his photography. After evaluating the results, Madan would send back a note along with the prints. On May 17, 1990, Madan received a roll of film from him wrapped in a note which read, "Madan, this is definitely _the_ last. I have even taken out the cells from the camera. Thanks. Love, Charan Singh." After processing the film, Madan wrote back to him saying: "The results for this time of year are amazingly good. Please put the batteries back into the camera and carry on shooting." But alas ...

Loving Regards
Charan Sin
Sewa Das

546

May your Love of the Form
Culminates in the Love of the Formless.
Love
Charan Sigh